LoveEd
LEVEL 2

BOYS THAT ARE STRONG, SMART AND PURE

LoveEd

LEVEL 2

BOYS THAT ARE STRONG, SMART AND PURE

Nihil Obstat
Reverend John Balluff, STD
Censor Deputatus
April 29, 2016

Permission to Publish
Most Reverend Joseph Siegel, DD, STL
Vicar General
Diocese of Joliet
May 2, 2016

ISBN: 978-1-5051-0934-4

Published in the United States by
Saint Benedict Press
PO Box 410487
Charlotte, NC 28241
www.SaintBenedictPress.com

Printed in the United States of America

Contents

LoveEd: An Introduction for Parents

It's no secret that today's culture is confused about love and sex. Movies, television, the Internet, and music expose children at an early age to twisted perceptions of romance and relationships. In a culture that is morally adrift, parents need the right tools to help them navigate their children safely through the dangerous temptations and distorted perceptions of sexuality.

As you attend the *LoveEd* event and work through the rest of this book with your child at home, both of you will discover the amazing truth that human sexuality has a wonderful meaning and purpose. That vocational purpose is passed on from generation to generation for those who love God and seek to serve Him, and is fulfilled when a man and a woman create a new family on their wedding day. In this family circle, children will learn how to love God, others, and themselves. *LoveEd* will help parents guide their children through the circles of love: *God's love, family love, friendship love, and an understanding of a future romantic love.*

By reading this book with their parents, children will learn that:

- God has made them to be a loving human person, both body and soul.
- God has planned for them to go through physical changes called puberty.
- God has called them to be strong, smart, and pure throughout their lives.
- God has created them to receive His love and share this amazing and pure love with others.

Level 2 of *LoveEd* will review the physical changes that occur during puberty and how these begin to prepare children for adulthood. In addition, it will explain the male and female powers to co-create life with God, how a child is created through God's natural and supernatural plan, and how a baby grows in the mother's womb from conception to birth. The Parent Training Event and accompanying *Parent Guide* provide you with additional information to assist you in communicating these sacred messages to your child and answering other related questions that may arise over time.

However, it is not enough for children to know about bodily functions. Human beings are much more than biological cells and systems—we are persons made in God's image! Working through this *LoveEd* program will give you the tools you need to teach, from a Christ-centered perspective, about some of the important changes that will be going on in your children's lives during the next few years, as well as the vital connection between their development of virtues and their vocation to love. When virtues are practiced, especially chastity, it can lead your children to a life of self-giving love and truly prepare them for adulthood.

Your children have the right and responsibility to know

information about their growth, which is both biological and spiritual. God's special plan for sexuality is best discussed in a personal conversation with you in the context of sound Church teaching. Attending this event and reading this book will help you and your children start the conversations that will help them understand themselves and their place in God's plan.

LoveEd can be the beginning, or the continuation, of those ongoing conversations with your children about life, love, and purity, conversations that can extend into their adulthood. It's important, now more than ever, for you to guide them while they develop a holy awe of God's amazing creation of life!

New to LoveEd?

This book is the second in the *LoveEd* series for boys. The first event and book were for preteens, around the fifth grade. The preteen program covered the basic elements of love and virtue, as well as the science and morality needed for puberty and the changes it brings. Human psychology affirms the Church teachings that tell us it is best for children to have a gradual education in human sexuality, beginning when they are young. *LoveEd* is here to give your son that teaching in conjunction with your involvement. That's right, you are going to be a big part of this journey your son is on. For this reason, *LoveEd* includes a Parent Training Event and accompanying *Parent Guide* that will help you learn what to say when all those teachable moments come up.

Hopefully, even if you didn't participate in the first part of *LoveEd*, you have in some way helped lay some kind of foundation for your son in teaching him about God's plan for his life. If you believe he understands how his body is changing and how a man of virtue responds to those changes, you're ready for this next level that includes the marriage union and the beginnings of life. If you are not sure, there is no harm in going back to do Level 1 of the program, even though your son may be past the intended age.

In conversations with your son, it's important to be in tune with what he already knows, what misperceptions he may have, and how well he understands the beauty of God's plan and its spiritual dimension. It's helpful to admit that he has picked up on various messages along the way from friends or the media, and then help him clarify the beauty of the whole truth and recognize the errors that keep so many people searching for love in all the wrong places. Give him goodness and truth so that he can become strong, smart, and pure!

PART I

Parent/Child Event

Complete the following six Acts by watching each video and answering the discussion questions with your Dad.

ACT 1

The Story of You

Introduction

The first Act introduces us to
an eighth grade boy named
Michael Sullivan, as well as his family and friends. We will
see him in his daily life and watch as he handles some of
the struggles that come with being a teenager.

 Watch Act 1

Father and Son Discussion

1. How is the Sullivan family similar to your family? How is
    it different?

_____

_____

_____

2. Tell your Dad something you like or dislike about Michael. Discuss how he is similar to you and how he is different.

_____

_____

_____

_____

3. Mr. Sullivan tells Michael that he needs integrity now that he is older. Work with your Dad to write a short definition for this word. Discuss how the word applies to your life and relationships.

Integrity: _____

_____

_____

_____

4. What are three ways your friendships with boys are different from your friendships with girls? Ask your Dad to tell you about his own friendships with boys and girls when he was growing up and what advice he has for you about this.

_____

_____

_____

_____

In anticipation of viewing the Act 2 video, please complete the following activity.

At the center of the circle named "Family," write the names of the people in your immediate family and/or those who live in your home. On the outside edge of that circle, write the names of other close family members, such as grandparents and close cousins or relatives you see often and love very much.

At the center of the circle named "Friends," write the names of your closest or favorite friends. On the outside edge of that circle, write the names of other kids you hang around with.

In the next Act, we'll learn about the third dotted circle and how you can prepare to enter it as well.

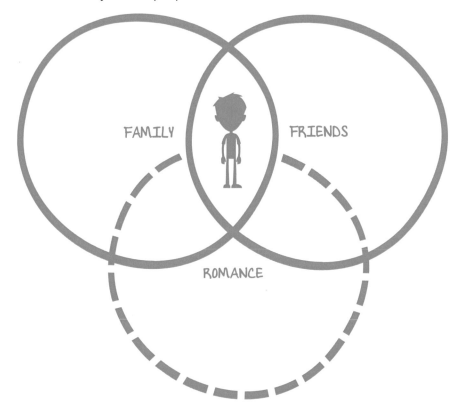

Affirming the Good

Ask your Dad to tell you about a time he was proud of you. Have him write it down so you can read it later.

_____

_____

_____

_____

_____

_____

_____

_____

_____

_____

_____

_____

_____

_____

ACT 2

Growing in Circles, Growing in Love

Introduction

The second Act has some important things to tell you about the three circles in our diagram and about God's plan for you and your life.

 Watch Act 2

Father and Son Discussion

1. You belong in your family. You belong in your friendship groups. And you belong to God. Your challenge is to reflect God's love in all three areas. How does your family expect you to act? How do your friends expect you to act? Do your own decisions and actions reflect God's love?

Below is a list of virtuous actions. Using a scale of 1 (low) to 5 (high):

- Rate each virtue action based on how important it is in your family.
- Rate each virtue action based on how important it is to your friends.
- In the last column, have your Dad rank how well you are doing (in all areas of your life) with that particular virtue action.

VIRTUE ACTION	FAMILY (1-5)	FRIENDS (1-5)	YOU (1-5)
Being polite			
Studying hard			
Being a good example			
Being kind to unpopular kids			
Telling the truth			
Respecting adults			
Respecting girls and boys			
Playing fair			
Practicing self-control			
Offering help when needed			
Praying at home and church			
Being trustworthy			
Apologizing for hurting someone			
Forgiving when you've been hurt			
Making good decisions on your own			

2. Review the chart with your Dad.

- What virtue actions had inconsistencies between how your family values it versus how your friends value it? Why do you suppose that is?

_____

_____

  - Which virtue actions did your Dad rate you highly on? Which ones does he want you to work harder at?

  _____

  _____

  - In general, was your Dad's ranking of your behavior in the last column closer to what your family values or to what your friends value?

  _____

  _____

3. Below you will find the definition of the virtue of **chastity** that was used in the video. Have your Dad read the definition to you, and ask him to explain it in his own words.

> Chastity is the virtue that directs our sexuality and sexual desires toward authentic love and away from using others as objects of sexual pleasure.
>
> Catechetical Formation in Chaste Living, USCCB, 2008

4. The virtue of chastity builds on the foundation of many of the other virtues you are learning to practice in your family and friendship circles. You will find three columns of virtues below. Have your Dad circle at least five that you will need to practice now in order to have healthy romantic relationships someday.

The word "virtue" here is meant to encompass "character strengths." These words describe the many areas of human goodness.

Love Requires Virtue

FAMILY VIRTUES	PERSONAL VIRTUES	FRIENDSHIP VIRTUES
Respect	Faith	Cooperation
Sharing	Modesty	Humility
Obedience	Good Judgment	Leadership
Caring	Integrity	Fairness
Patience	Compassion	Independence
Forgiveness	Confidence	Trust
Gratitude	Courage	Confidence
Helpfulness	Self-Denial	Honesty
Responsibility	Chastity	Courtesy
Truthfulness	Competence	Teamwork
Kindness	Initiative	Goodness
Courage	Thoughtfulness	Self-Control

5. Discuss ways you can practice the virtues your Dad circled.

Affirming the Good

1. Dad, when do you see me being a loving member of our family?

_____

_____

_____

_____

2. Dad, I notice that you're teaching our family to love when you:

_____

_____

_____

_____

ACT 3

God's Story . . . From the Beginning

Introduction

Act 3 zooms out to God's view of the universe and helps us learn that everything we are and everything we have is a gift of God's creative love. Watch carefully in the video for some pictures of Bible stories that show God's love.

 Watch Act 3

Father and Son Discussion

Listed below are some quotes from the video. Read them with your Dad and discuss the questions.

1. "God made the whole world, and He made it amazing." Name some of the things in God's world that you think are amazing.

_____

_____

_____

2. "God made fish to swim, animals to run, and planets to circle the sun." What did He make us human beings to do?

_____

_____

_____

3. "God gives every human being two great gifts that make us capable of loving—the ability to know and understand (intellect) and the power to make free choices (free will)." In what ways do human beings misuse these gifts?

_____

_____

_____

4. "Sin is a choice to turn away from God. Sinful choices tear families apart, ruin friendships, and corrupt romantic relationships." Discuss some of the unloving choices that can cause these bad consequences.

_____

_____

_____

5. "When we are children, our parents try to protect us from all harmful things." What are some of the ways your parents have tried to protect you from evil? Ask

your Dad to help you think of these ways, and have him explain why he and your Mom did these things.

_____

_____

_____

6. "When we sin, God always gives us another chance to come home to Him and ask for forgiveness." Remember together the parable of the Prodigal Son. (If you need help, look up Lk 15:11–32.) What does Jesus teach us in this story about God's loving mercy?

_____

_____

_____

7. "When we are wounded by another person's sin, God sends someone to bring us the healing power of His love." Remember together the parable of the Good Samaritan (Lk 10:25–37). What does Jesus teach us in this story about how to care for people who are suffering?

_____

_____

_____

8. Write down three words that come to mind when you think of Jesus's crucifixion and resurrection. Then have your Dad write down three new words. Compare and discuss.

My words:

_____

_____

_____

Dad's words:

_____

_____

_____

9. The video ends by saying, "Now it is our turn to help create a more loving world." Name some of the ways you and your family are trying to do this.

_____

_____

_____

Affirming the Good

Dad, you can see that I love God when I

_____

_____

_____

_____

_____

Dad, I can see that you love God when you

_____

_____

_____

_____

_____

ACT 4

The Science of Life

Introduction

Act 4 will explain sexual development in both men and women, as well as the process by which a new life is created and developed in the mother's body.

 Watch Act 4

Father and Son Discussion

1. Review the male anatomy diagram with your Dad and answer these questions. This will help you understand what's going on inside your body. Use the following answer key: A. testicle, B. penis, C. scrotum, D. sperm.

   The _____ is a soft sac that holds the two testicles just outside the male body.

   The _____ is a small ball-shaped organ that produces male hormones.

The _____ is the male organ through which both urine and semen can pass.

The _____ are the male reproductive cells.

Male
Anatomy
Diagram

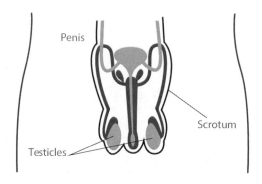

Female
Anatomy
Diagram

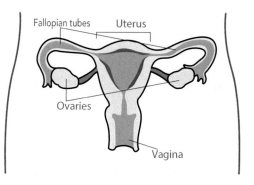

2. Review the female anatomy diagram with your Dad and answer these questions. Use the following answer key: A. Uterus or womb, B. vagina, C. fallopian tube, D. ovary. *One of these letters is used twice.*

The _____ releases an egg cell once a month.

The _____ is also called the birth canal.

The _____ is the tunnel through which the egg cell travels.

The _____ holds the menstrual blood until the end of the month.

The _____ surrounds the baby when a mom is pregnant.

3. List three changes you've seen in your body in the last year.

   _____

   _____

   _____

4. The video also presented some of the emotional and mental changes that take place during puberty. Ask your Dad for a few examples of changes he has seen in you recently, and how you can manage these changing emotions.

My Dad has seen the following emotional and/or behavioral changes in me:

_____

_____

_____

I will try to manage these changes better by:

_____

_____

_____

5. Ask your Dad to review what the video said about the marriage act between a man and a woman (sexual intercourse). Ask any questions you might have, especially if you think you have learned some misinformation from friends or anywhere else in society.

_____

_____

_____

6. The video explains conception by saying, "The moment the egg and sperm join together, God infuses a soul and a new human person is created." Talk with your Dad about this amazing miracle. What was it like for him and your Mom when they realized that the miracle of new life had happened in her womb?

_____

_____

_____

7. The video says, "The life of this person should be honored and protected from this moment (conception) until natural death." This is a basic teaching of the Catholic Church: abortion kills a human person. Talk to

your Dad about some of the things that Catholics do in your church or diocese to help stop abortion.

Here is something you can do for the pro-life cause: Finish by doing a "spiritual adoption" where you pray for the intention of a baby in danger of being aborted by his mother and father.

Spiritual Adoption Prayer

Think about a child who is on the verge of being aborted. Silently pray for that baby and for the baby's father and mother. *"Jesus, Mary and Joseph, I love you very much. I beg you to spare the life of this unborn baby that I have spiritually adopted who is in danger of abortion."*

Prayer given to us by Archbishop Fulton Sheen

ACT 5

The Journey towards Love

Introduction

Act 5 helps you learn how to live God's love as a teenager and adult. You will learn some tips on how to become *strong* in your decisions, *smart* in your knowledge of life, and *pure* in your thoughts and actions. Listen for the good news that there are many people who are here to help you along this journey.

 Watch Act 5

Father and Son Discussion

The goal of *LoveEd* has been to encourage you to be *smart*, *strong*, and *pure* as you learn to manage your sexual feelings and desires according to God's plan. The first exercise below will help you to review how much you have learned and understood with your *intellect*. The second exercise can help you know how to strengthen your *will*.

Understanding Life and Love (with my Intellect)

Listed below are ten important facts about sex and sexuality. Read each item to your Dad and mark it with one of the following signs:

✝ A plus sign means you understand it and accept how important it is. You can use two or three plus signs if you find it especially important. Tell your Dad why.

❓ A question mark means something about it is still not clear to you.

☐ God created you for love. Your whole purpose in life is to love God and to love others. God also wants you to love and care for yourself.

☐ God has given you an intellect and a will, the two great human powers that make you capable of love. As you mature, you must *learn* to love and *choose* to love.

☐ When you truly love someone, you want what is best for the other person, not only what is best for yourself.

☐ You learn to love in your family and in your friendship circles by practicing virtues like respect, patience, courage, gratitude, forgiveness, and honesty.

☐ Sexual attraction and sexual desire, which begin during adolescence, cause you to be interested in girls and see their bodies as beautiful.

☐ Marriage is a solemn vow to God by which a man and a woman promise to love and care for one another until death.

☐ Sexual intercourse has a double purpose: the loving union of a man and a woman in marriage and the creation and raising of children.

☐ Sexual intercourse is meant by God to be a sign (a sacrament) of the love of the married man and woman. Outside of marriage, sex is a sin.

☐ Sexual activity outside of marriage is called lust. Lustful sex will never bring happiness; rather, it will cause many problems not only for the two people involved but also for many others.

☐ Songs, movies, and TV shows often portray sex as lust. If you watch and listen to such things over and over, you will begin to see them as normal.

Making One Good Choice after Another (with my Free Will)

In order to be spiritually *strong* and *pure*, you need to practice virtue. You acquire virtues by making one good choice after another. Listed below are some *good choices* that will help you become a responsible and loving adult. You can make these choices, with the helping grace of God, as you follow His plan for you to choose real love.

Read each item with your Dad and mark it with one of the following signs.

✝ A plus sign means you understand it and accept how important it is. You can use two or three plus signs if you find it especially important. Tell your Dad why.

❓ A question mark means something about it is still not clear to you.

☐ When I have questions about sex, I will ask my parents, church leaders, and other morally trusted adults—not my peers or the Internet.

☐ I will follow the guidance of my parents concerning sexuality, parties, dating, and entertainment.

☐ I will choose friends who have positive values regarding sexuality, love, and marriage.

☐ I will develop good friendships with many girls: talking with them, getting to know them, doing class assignments and projects with them, and planning wholesome fun events with them.

☐ I will avoid using alcohol and drugs—substances that will weaken or destroy my ability to make good choices.

☐ I will avoid pornography—pictures, shows, songs, texts, or jokes that present people's bodies and sexual relationships in a lustful or disrespectful way.

☐ I will pray every day for the grace to be a loving person and to make the many good choices I need to be morally strong.

☐ I will go to Mass every week and really participate in the prayers and singing.

☐ I will go to confession often, telling the priest about any sinful choices I have made and promising to make better choices in the future.

☐ I will try to remember that Jesus walks with me every minute of every day, always encouraging me to be the best, most loving person I can be.

Now walk through this map with your Dad and review the meaning of each little icon.

Map from the Journey towards Love Video

List one message that resonated with you as you watched Act 5:

_____

_____

_____

Affirming the Good

1. Dad, you see that I am being spiritually strong when I

_____

_____

_____

2. Dad, you see that I am being smart about my manhood when I

_____

_____

_____

3. Dad, you see that I am committed to being pure when I

_____

_____

_____

Finish by telling your Dad when he most helps you become strong, smart, and pure.

_____

_____

_____

Planning Time to be with my Dad

Before you begin the final Act, fill in the following with each other to make a commitment with your Dad to work together on Part II of the program. You will be reading each chapter and answering discussion questions with your Dad.

Dad, let's plan *now* when we will finish Part II of this *LoveEd* program at home.

The best day of the week for us to spend time alone together is _____ .

The best time of day for us to spend time alone together is _____ .

The best place for us to spend time alone together is _____ .

Let's plan to do . . .

Chapter 1 on _____ at _____ o'clock

Chapter 2 on _____ at _____ o'clock.

Chapter 3 on _____ at _____ o'clock.

Chapter 4 on _____ at _____ o'clock.

Chapter 5 on _____ at _____ o'clock.

Chapter 6 on _____ at _____ o'clock.

Thanks, Dad!

To complete Part II of the program, you will need to read each chapter before meeting with your Dad.

ACT 6

Prayer and Blessing Ceremony

This final Act in *LoveEd* leads us back to God our Father who loves us. By now we all know that we need God's grace in order to love well. Jesus, as a young adolescent, was determined to follow God's will.

In lieu of a video for Act 6, with fathers and sons together, read and discuss the Bible story of Jesus with His parents in the temple at age twelve (Lk 2:41–52). Focus on the last part of the passage that says Jesus was "obedient" to his parents and that he "advanced in wisdom and age and favor before God and man."

Discuss why it is important to always obey your parents, as well as God the Father, in order to grow in wisdom and in grace.

Once your discussion is complete, each father and son will read a prayer of blessing for each other.

A Parent's Blessing

God, our Father and Creator,
You have entrusted to me the life of [name] as a gift from
You.
He is a gift to our family and to the world.
Thank You for him.

As [name] moves through his adolescent years,
may he continue to grow, as young Jesus did,
in wisdom, strength, and grace.

Beloved God, guide him each day
as he makes his life a gift of love,
to You and to all people.
Help [name] be strong, smart, and pure,
and full of faith, hope, and love.

God, I ask Your blessing on my dear son.
Pour out Your grace on him and draw him close to You.
Through Christ our Lord.
Amen.

A Son's Prayer for His Father

God, our Father and Creator,
I thank You for my Dad.
Bless him with Your great love and mercy.
Help him to be the best father he can be:
a man of virtue and strength.
Give him the courage and faith he needs to
teach me and guide me
so that we both may do Your will and create
a more loving world.
Amen.

PART II

At-Home Follow-Up

Once you get home from the Event, work through these six chapters at the time you and your Dad planned. They will help you review the information found in the videos and provide more ideas about educating yourself for real love. Answer the questions after each chapter and discuss your answers with your Dad so he can help you discover practical ways to live these lessons.

CHAPTER 1

Changing Here, Changing Now

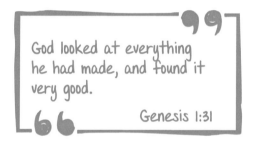

> God looked at everything
> he had made, and found it
> very good.
>
> Genesis 1:31

There are days when you envy your dog . . .

You know you're having a bad day when you envy your dog. Middle school may hold the record in a guy's life for the most days of dog envy. You wish you could just veg out on the porch, lie in the sun, have someone else clean up your poop, not go to school, and not have someone bothering you about wearing a jacket when *they* think it's cold (when you know it's not cold). You wish you could run with your friends when you want and spend a lot of alone time whenever you choose.

Michael envies his dog because his dog doesn't have

parents to obey. The dog doesn't have to answer to a family or set a good example for a little brother. Age fourteen is certainly dogging poor Mike.

With the possible exception of wanting someone to scoop up your droppings, you might identify with Michael. Look at your family picture from just a couple years ago. Dad looks pretty much the same, maybe a little chubbier now. Mom has a different hairstyle, maybe new glasses; that's about it, though she'll tell you she looks way older now because of details you don't even notice. Your baby brother or sister just looks more babyish.

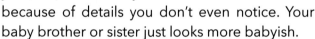

But you! You wouldn't let your friends see that picture. You look like a little kid. You don't even know who that kid is now. You don't like the same music anymore. You don't play the same games anymore (or at least you don't admit to it in public). All this growing-up-and-becoming-a-man stuff you used to imagine is pretty much happening. And it pretty much stinks.

Yeah, a dog's life seems pretty good some days.

You know you're not a kid anymore, but you wish you were. Being a kid again would maybe even be better than being a dog. You don't have a care in the world when you're a kid. Just get carried around, yell for food when you're hungry, and then throw it when you're ticked off. No list of household chores for you to tackle. No lawn to help mow. No lame books to read for a program at church or school.

On the other hand, growing up has its perks. You're taller. You're starting, even if ever so slightly, to bulk up.

You have way more endurance. Your personal bests in fifth grade don't even make you break a sweat now. Kids around town are starting to talk about driving in a few years. And if you have a fun big brother who was once your personal jungle gym and you thought the world of him for it, you're now seeing that you can be that for your younger siblings. But most days, nah–you wonder if it's all worth it.

Your friends are changing, too. You probably have at least one friend who's started to shave, and you swear they'd better check his house's water for hormones. You went back to school and someone grew half a foot over the summer and went from sounding like a kid to sounding like the Hulk after an anger-management fail.

And something else you might have noticed (if you haven't been living under a rock) is that the girls your age are changing. The way you feel about them is changing, too, and you can't change the changes. Being a guy can be tough these days.

All of this makes you wish that, just for today, you could be a baby or a dog.

"And There Was Light"

If you ask your Mom or Dad, they've probably seen (or at least heard of) a musical called *Les Misérables*. Maybe you've seen it. It's the story of some students rebelling against the French government in Paris in the 1830s–not the French Revolution, but one of the many small aftershocks. You probably hate musicals, but this one is pretty good. The musical is based on a novel that's about twelve hundred pages long and is written by a French author named Victor Hugo.

In a cast of many characters, there's a student named

Marius (probably just a bit older than you) and a girl named Cosette who is around fifteen. Amid the revolt and Cosette's stepfather getting pursued by the police because he is really an escaped convict, the two of them find the time to have feelings for each other. If you think Michael's dilemma about staying with Julia at a party or leaving to take care of his little brother is a tight spot, try starting a relationship while getting shot at behind a barricade by the French army.

But it's not like this was something Marius was looking for. He used to go to a park in Paris and walk; it was just a place to reflect and clear his head. This was before iPads, so he had to walk on a path or sit on park benches and actually think before meeting up with his friends (who were slowly planning an armed rebellion). Well, Marius would often see this old man and a girl he assumed was his young daughter sitting on a park bench. He saw them every day, every time he walked. Then for some reason, he didn't see them for a while.

You're a smart kid, so you can handle the real deal. Maybe twelve hundred pages of Victor Hugo is too much right now, but you can tackle one or two:

> He went straight to "his alley," and when he reached the end of it he perceived, still on the same bench, that well-known couple. Only, when he approached, it certainly was the same man; but it seemed to him that it was no longer the same girl. The person whom he now beheld was a tall and beautiful creature, possessed of all the most charming lines of a woman at the precise moment when they are still combined with all the most ingenuous graces of the child; a pure and fugitive moment, which can be expressed only by these two words, "fifteen years."

She had wonderful brown hair, shaded with threads of gold, a brow that seemed made of marble, cheeks that seemed made of rose-leaf, a pale flush, an agitated whiteness, an exquisite mouth, whence smiles darted like sunbeams, and words like music, a head such as [Italian painter] Raphael would have given to Mary, set upon a neck that [French sculptor] Jean Goujon would have attributed to a Venus. And, in order that nothing might be lacking to this bewitching face, her nose was not handsome–it was pretty; neither straight nor curved, neither Italian nor Greek; it was the Parisian nose, that is to say, spiritual, delicate, irregular, pure–which drives painters to despair, and charms poets.

When Marius passed near her, he could not see her eyes, which were constantly lowered. He saw only her long chestnut lashes, permeated with shadow and modesty.

This did not prevent the beautiful child from smiling as she listened to what the white-haired old man was saying to her, and nothing could be more fascinating than that fresh smile, combined with those drooping eyes.

For a moment, Marius thought that she was another daughter of the same man, a sister of the former, no doubt. But when the invariable habit of his stroll brought him, for the second time, near the bench, and he had examined her attentively, he recognized her as the same. In six months the little girl had become a young maiden; that was all. Nothing is more frequent than this phenomenon. There is a moment when girls blossom out in the twinkling of an eye, and become roses all at once. One left them

children but yesterday; today, one finds them dis-
quieting to the feelings.

This child had not only grown, she had become
idealized. As three days in April suffice to cover certain trees with flowers, six months had sufficed to
clothe her with beauty. Her April had arrived.

Victor Hugo wrote at a time when writers had all day to write
for people who had all day to read. But you get the picture. The *Cliff Notes* version? Marius looks at her and thinks,
"Wow! Now I see her beauty that I never noticed in the past!"

The young girl he used to see is now a young woman.
The author entitled the chapter *"Et Lux Facta Est,"* which is
Latin for that famous verse in the creation story in the Book
of Genesis, *"*. . . and there was light" (Gn 1:3).

Marius suddenly is rocked by new feelings he was not
expecting. He loses track of time and shows up late to meet
his friends.

In the musical, when Marius's friends hassle him for
being late, he sings about his overwhelming feelings and
how he was struck by Cosette's beauty. It seemed as if his
whole outlook on life changed.

Marius is experiencing something he has never felt
before. He thinks he may be experiencing something
nobody has ever felt before. And so will you. If not already,
you will, sooner or later.

So is Michael. He thinks about Julia all the time. *She's pretty, she's smart, she's good at sports, she's funny, and whenever I see her, my heart starts pounding . . . and I'm an idiot.*

Victor Hugo used that chapter title for a reason. It shows that the beauty of such a moment is like the beauty of the first thing God ever made: light itself. It also shows that this story is related to and is as old as creation itself.

The video told the story of Michael and his chat at the cookout with Julia. Michael has known Julia for a while. They grew up as neighbors and have been friends for a while. But he's experiencing feelings for her that he has never felt before. He's eager to know if she feels the same.

Yet, part of him doesn't want to know how she feels, on the chance that she may not be feeling the same way. The

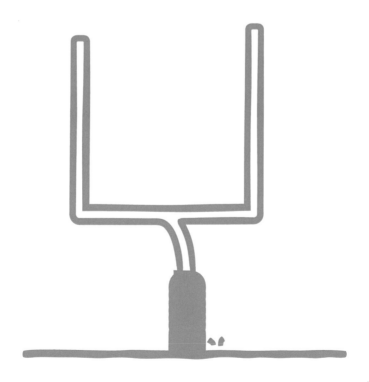

last thing he wants to think about is having to rush home to obey his parents. But he knows he must. How can he ever explain how he feels to them, anyway? They are the same as they have ever been, but his world is spinning in circles.

The purpose of this book is to help you sort out those circles. If you can in any way identify with Michael or Marius, if you've ever envied your baby brother or your dog, if you've ever secretly loved the way your burps smell after two bags of Doritos, this book is for you. You'll read it along with (not necessarily out loud though) your parents—preferably your Dad since your Mom just shrieked at that Doritos thing (but then again she can't stand the smell of your room for more than thirty seconds). Reading the book together is *not* meant to be a form of torture or embarrassment. Your Dad has been through all those spinning circles and has lived to tell the tale.

In the remaining chapters of this book, let's try to put these spinning circles in order. We'll see that they are part of God's plan—a plan for love, a plan for life. This plan is visible in nature around us, as well as in the natural changes we go through, which are most evident at your age. But there is a deeper plan here, part of God's secret design for saving the world (way better than a minor rebellion in Paris). And what is most important is to recognize how you can live through all these changes and fulfill God's plan for you. Like the scribbles of a great coach, the circles and changes are the X's and O's of God's amazing game plan for your life. Victory is assured if you execute His playbook!

So whether you're secretly interested in the rest of this book, or are going through this kicking and screaming, ask for God's help either way and get ready for the rest of it. But first, check and see whether you need to watch your little brother or walk the dog.

Discussion Questions

Answer and discuss these questions with your Dad.

1. Go find a picture in your house of your family from at least four years ago. How do your family members look different now than they used to? How are they alike?

2. Name a boy you know who has changed a lot in the last three years—your brother, cousin, neighbor, or a friend. How is he different?

3. Write down three things you've noticed about yourself that have changed in the last few years. Your interests? Your size? Likes and dislikes?

4. Write down three changes you've noticed in the last few years with your friendships:

_____

_____

_____

Chapter Reflections

While discussing this chapter, my Dad gave me some extra advice about . . .

_____

_____

_____

While reading this chapter, I learned these two important things:

1. _____

2. _____

I resolve to live out the *LoveEd* teachings from this chapter by . . .

_____

_____

_____

Finish this chapter with the following prayer:

Lord, thank You for my family and my friends, for the good times and the bad. Give me guidance to understand myself, my family, and others as we enter our teenage years. Help us all to love one another as You love us. Amen.

My Dad and I completed this chapter on

_____

(date and time)

CHAPTER 2

Circles of Life, Circles of Virtue

> **"**
> We must consider how
> to rouse one another to love
> and good works.
>
> Hebrews 10:24
> **66**

In the middle of a field on a summer night, you can see more stars than you could count before the sun came up. A space ship recently visited Pluto at the edge of our solar system, arriving after ten years and three *billion* miles! Three billion miles is just a drop in the bucket, given the size of our universe.

It's easy to get overwhelmed when we think how small we really are in all of this. And yet God made it all, and God knows it all, and God cares for it all. It was His choice, His yes that made everything. He loved things into existence. It blows your mind to think of how awesome that is, doesn't it?

Think of David, whom God called to defeat Goliath, watching the stars on a summer night long ago. His mind was a bit blown by all of that as well, and he wrote about this in one of his psalms: "Even before a word is on my tongue, / LORD, you know it all. / Behind and before you encircle me / and rest your hand upon me. / Such knowledge is too wonderful for me, / far too lofty for me to reach. / Where can I go from your spirit? / From your presence, where can I flee?" (Ps 139:4-7).

God's plan can be represented by three circles. These circles are actually found within an even greater circle: the circle of God's love, which surrounds and gives grace to these three circles that you are (or will be) a part of your life. There is no way of escaping it. And hey, why would you want to?

Inside this great circle—the circle of God's love, the circle of God, who *is* love—we live our lives. St. Paul, trying to explain this to the Greeks, quoted one of their poets who said, "In him we live and move and have our being" (Acts 17:28). Everything we are and will ever be is inside this immense circle.

God created us to love Him. We love Him by loving what He loves and returning this love to Him by being the best we can be. We will live forever in this love in heaven. He created us to be with Him forever!

But who are we and what will we be? The question

"Who am I?" has many answers. Michael is a son, a brother, a friend, and more. Inside this immense circle of God's love, our lives unfold in other circles of love, where love is defined as is sacrificing ourselves for the good of others.

The Family Circle

FAMILY

We came into this world through God's love, but also through the love of our parents. Our family is a fundamental circle of love for us. It's unique to each of us. Even if you come from a big family, there is only one oldest child and one second child, for instance. If you have two brothers and two sisters, nobody else in your family has the same two brothers and two sisters as you! Whether you're an only child, have one pestering sister, or are one of a zillion cousins, your family is the place you first learn to love and be loved. Your family is unique, and your place in your family is unique.

God wants every child He creates to be brought up in a loving family circle where he or she will be loved and cared for at every minute. It doesn't always work that way though, does it?

We know that every family has its challenges: Some are single-parent families, some are blended families, and even those families with parents still married to each other don't always agree on every issue. Some families do not have children, some have children with disabilities, some have children they were blessed to adopt, and some have

children that do not live with them. In all families there are many others who are an important part of the family love circle—grandparents, aunts and uncles, older brothers and sisters, cousins, and sometimes friends and babysitters. No family is perfect, but God wants each family to be responsible to love and care for each other, especially the children.

In your family, maybe you're the one who is smart and likes spicy food, or the musician who prefers ranch dressing. Or maybe you're the one with the best dance moves who likes pizza (but never with mushrooms). The possibilities are as endless as the stars we couldn't count before. Even if you're an identical twin, there is nobody else *exactly* like you!

And the love your parents have for you is also unique. Your parents' love is a response to the unique gift that you are in the family, with your unique set of traits and possibilities and talents and quirks. And that love reflects God's unique love in creating you. We were not created in an assembly line, "cookie-cutter style." We are each hand-crafted, so to speak, by God Himself. No two treasure chests contain the same assortment of jewels.

God created the unique combination of traits that would make up our bodies and the even more unique nature of our souls. When we say we believe in God who created "all things visible and invisible," we speak of the amazing universe and the even more amazing invisible world that includes angels and our own souls.

Your grandmother may say you have your father's eyes or your Aunt Zoe's nose. You may very well share some similarity with them. (I hope Aunt Zoe has a nice nose!) But Grandma and you both know that your nose is your nose and your eyes are your eyes. Your DNA is your own, although a scientist can prove that you are related to your family members.

But you're more than your DNA. You also have your heavenly Father's mind and heart. You share in His ability to know and love. This image of God in your soul is the root of your dignity as a person, and nobody can ever take it from you. When we learn the truth and exercise our will by doing good things to form virtuous habits, we are living out this dignity and showing God's image to the world.

When players on a team execute their coach's plan and win a victory, they honor his hard work, and he is in his glory. We respond to God's love and glorify Him by being who He created us to be. He is glorified when His plan is fulfilled. And since we are His plan, He is glorified when we are fulfilled.

God created you to be a gift to your family and your family to be a gift to you. It may not always feel like it, because living in a family can be tough. But it's precisely that toughness that is part of the gift, even though it seems crazy to think of it that way. You can drive down the highway and pass huge cornfields basking in the sun, with farmers sweating from the heat moving in and out of the giant stalks. The long, hot summer days that are so tough on these farmers are exactly what their corn needs to grow. The struggles we have obeying our parents and being patient with our siblings can also be rough, but they are precisely what *we* need to grow. One reason God gave us a family, no matter what that family looks like, is so we can learn the virtues that will make us better at loving other people—and loving God most of all. When we get better at obeying our parents, we will be better at obeying God. When we are kind to our family members, we will be more charitable to other people for the love of God.

The family circle, then, is a first circle of love and virtue. We have a great opportunity to grow and practice virtue each day as part of a family. Virtues are like spiritual muscles—you need to exercise them in every situation of life. Just think of all these different virtues and the opportunities you have each day to practice them:

- Respect
- Sharing
- Obedience
- Caring
- Patience
- Forgiveness
- Gratitude
- Helpfulness

You may not like it all the time, but you can't deny that being a member of a family is a workout in the gym of virtue. Practicing these virtues is a gift you give to God for the gift of love He gave you within your family.

Think about it—your family came from other families. Your parents learned about love in their own families, and when they formed a new family, those learned virtues and lessons came with them. Our human world is made up of smaller circles within the circles of love.

You're already old enough to know that your relationship to your family has changed. You aren't as absorbed in your family as you were when you were a baby. You know people your own age who aren't members of your family. You share common interests, you play together, and you even share inside jokes. This is a new circle in your life, one that is very important. It's the circle of friendship.

The Friendship Circle

You don't choose your parents or your siblings, but you do choose your friends. Of course, the first Person to make sure you develop a lifelong friendship with is Jesus. He will be with you your whole life, 24/7/365, ready to listen, guide, comfort, and get you through any and every blessing and challenge that may come your way.

But in life there will be people you choose to get closer to for a million different reasons: you like the same football team, have the same taste in music, share a similar fashion sense, practice the same religious beliefs, or study the same favorite subject in school. The love that friends share is real love for each other, and it often stems from a shared love of something. True friendship means loving your friends, but it also means loving some of the same things together with them.

It can be very comforting to know that a friend is feeling the same way I am when my team wins or is laughing for the same reason I am at the same silly video. Think of your friends and what you enjoy together. You may have even grown to love something new because of the influence of a friend.

As you grow, you may start to feel closer to your friends than to your family. In one way this is impossible since your family will always be your family. But in another way it's understandable because we won't live with our families forever. Even though it's still a few years down the road, nature inside us prepares us to leave the nest. Our circle of friends becomes like a new flock for us.

This is also part of God's plan, and it all happens inside the big circle of His love. But since He chooses our family for us and we choose our friends, we have to choose friends wisely. Love means wanting what is best for someone, and

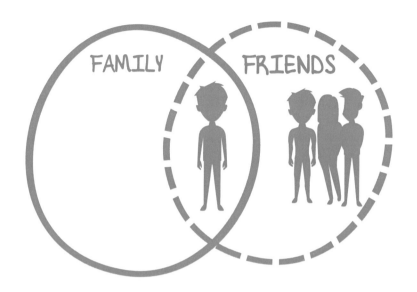

if your friends aren't helping you to love God more, they're probably not the best choice you could make. Just as the family is a school of virtue, friendship is, too. And a very important first virtue to form is the habit of choosing the right kind of friends. A true friend wants what is best for you and will never pressure you to do something that's bad for you.

The circle of friendship includes other virtues that you exercise when you strive to be a good friend:

- Cooperation
- Compromise
- Leadership
- Fair play
- Wholesome fun
- Trust
- Kindness
- Honesty

It's simply not possible to be a good friend and not practice these virtues. Would you ever want to have a friend who was habitually uncooperative or whom you couldn't trust? Of course not!

Your parents are a great resource here. If you have struggles in your circle of friendship, fall back on your family circle for help. Older siblings can help, too. Chances are they've had similar struggles. Maybe they had to spend less time with a friend who wasn't good for them or had to talk through a misunderstanding with a friend. Never think you're being disloyal to a friend if you speak to your parents. The family circle came before your circle of friendship and is always more fundamental. And your best friends will most likely be the ones that are on best terms with your family.

The circle of friendship is the first circle beyond the family where we can grow in love for others and in wholesome love for ourselves, all within the bigger picture of our love for God.

In some ways, it's easier to think of God as the grand cosmic Creator rather than as a friend. The big circle is so big, it seems to suit God's bigness. You're probably used to hearing that your family circle is a gift from God, but it's hard sometimes to think of God caring about our little circle of friends.

The fact is, God took on a human nature so He could put us into *His* circle of friends and be welcomed into ours. Jesus wants to be our friend. When St. John, who met Jesus as a teenager, reflected as an old man about his life, he wanted to communicate the amazing mystery of having seen, heard, and clasped hands with this great God who became a man. And in John's Gospel, he refers to himself as "the disciple whom Jesus loved." Jesus chose him to be His friend.

On a day when you're feeling down or discouraged, you may think, *"Well, I can't be totally lame because my friend [name one!] is a great person and chose me to be a friend."* And even if you ever have a day when you feel like you can't name a single friend, you can always name Jesus, who is the most loyal friend we can ever have.

So the gift of love to God in our family continues in the gift of love to God through our friends. The circles grow and expand but can never outgrow the circle of God's love.

We said earlier that the circle of friendship includes a love of others and a shared love of other things. We give ourselves to our friends in our love for these other things. We should always put people before things, but it's also natural that, as our interests change, our circle of friends also shifts. Our best buds in one grade might not be our "besties" two years later. This is natural.

But we should always be open to loving everyone, even if we have little in common or do not enjoy a strong friendship with them. Like the members of your family, it was part of God's plan that you have this group of kids in your class and on your street and on your team and in your club. Each person you meet is a gift from God for you, and He has given them a gift in you as well. You should never be hurtful to anyone because of your friendship to someone else. That is not being the best version of yourself at all.

Though a group of friends may feel very close, it's still not the same thing as a family. A family comes from a special kind of love, a special kind of friendship. You can have many friends in your life, and you will be lucky if you have a few close friends that last for many years. But only one special kind of friendship will grow into a new family circle. This begins with a new type of circle, which we can call "the romance circle."

The Romance Circle

Do you know where and how your parents met? (Moms tend to remember these things with more details than dads, by the way.) Chances are they started out in the same circle of friends. They got to know each other because their families were friends or they had a similar circle of friends in school or at work. Perhaps their relationship was first fueled by a common interest. But *something* happened.

What happened was a spark that has been described in a million songs, poems, and movies, something that explodes into cards and chocolates and flying cupids on February 14 (which, by the way, is the feast day of a bishop named St. Valentine who gave his life for Christ). As you get older, your Mom or Dad may ask you, "Is so-and-so a friend or a *friend*?" and you'll know what they mean as you die of embarrassment.

Romantic attraction is a special kind of attraction that leads to special kind of friendship, a friendship that goes beyond a shared love of something (a hobby, sports team, music, etc.) to a shared life together as husband and wife. When this new circle comes from a strong friendship, the virtues formed from being a good friend are a good preparation for it. So there's no hurry or rush to find a special *friend* if you aren't solid in your other friendships. A strong character is essential to develop before entering into the circle of romantic love.

The circle of romantic love requires that you exercise these additional virtues:

- Self-control
- Modesty
- Chastity
- Purity
- Courtesy
- Truthfulness

If we're not honest, fair, kind, respectful, and so on, we will not be capable of managing ourselves, our emotions, or our relationships very well. Our relationships, without virtues, will be a disaster.

In the previous chapter, we saw an attraction between Michael and Julia. Although it's way too early to say, it's the type of attraction that could eventually lead to Michael and Julia getting married and giving themselves to each other for life. Romantic attraction might lead to real love, but it's not the same as love. That is very important to keep in mind.

Your friends are important, and you give yourself to them, but you don't give *a complete gift of self*. A complete gift of self is a gift you can give to one person only, and it's a commitment you make only once, even though you can renew this gift in little ways every day.

If you had a bucket of water and a series of other buckets, you could put part of the water into many other buckets, emptying it out little by little. But if you could turn the bucket over *only once*, there could *only be one bucket* you could pour it into. If there was a gift that had to be given whole, it could only go to one person. That is what is demanded by the word *whole*. In a similar way, you can only give your whole self to one person.

This makes the romantic circle very special. A romantic friendship is one that is focused toward a whole gift of self in marriage and family. Beyond the feelings and emotions involved—which are real and good and part of God's plan— the romantic circle is asking, "Is this the person I am going to give my whole self to?"

The struggles and virtues of the romantic circle are special, and they will be the focus of the rest of this book. The virtues formed in the family circle and the circle of friendship carry over into the romantic circle, because they will help form a new family circle, just as your parents brought the virtues of their own families to the new family that includes you.

Once you step into the circle of romantic love, those spiritual muscles that you've been working on will be more important than ever. In all your relationships with young women, you'll need to practice the virtues already mentioned, and more. But there's a special virtue that God wants you to pray for and work on starting *now*. It's called chastity. Chastity is the virtue that directs our sexuality and sexual energy toward authentic love and away from using people as objects of pleasure. The virtue of chastity will help you to keep your thoughts and experiences of romantic love pure and according to God's plan for you.

The subtitle title of this book helps summarize what we mean. You need to be *strong*. Just as there are struggles in the other two circles, there are often tougher ones in the romantic circle. You will need the strength of a hero to meet them. You need to be *smart*. You need to know the facts of God's plan, in the visible natural world and in the invisible realm of your soul, in order to live up to the greatness of His plan.

But you also need to be *pure*. That word may not sound as attractive as the others. Of course, no one wants to be a weakling and no one wants to be a moron, but what does purity have to do with the romantic circle? Everything!

We spoke about a complete gift of self. A whole gift. All you and nothing but you. In order to achieve that, you have to fight to be all that you can be. You want to give a gift of pure gold–*pure* gold–not a fraud or a cheat. A whole gift of self means a gift that is all you and only you. In other words, it's *pure* you.

When we speak about virtues such as purity, chastity, and modesty, they are the concrete demands of preparing ourselves for that gift of our whole selves. The virtue of chastity is a spiritual energy that will help you practice real love instead of selfishness. It will keep you from giving a fake, counterfeit gift, one that deep down is really just a fraud. Chastity leads to real love.

All of these circles are ways to respond to God for the great gift of His love. We love God by loving our family and practicing the virtues of family life. We love God by being a good and loyal friend to the many friends in our life. But we most reflect God's image in the total gift of ourselves to Him.

During these growing-up years, you may come to realize that you're being called to give your life to God as a priest, religious brother, or consecrated single person. If you say this type of yes to God, you will spend your whole life bringing God's love and care into the lives of others.

Giving yourself in a total gift to God takes a lot of work. In a sense, it is a longer journey than the ten years and three billion miles to get to Pluto. It is a huge trip, but little things are important. If the spaceship's course had been off even a small fraction of a degree, it would never have reached Pluto.

The good news is that the very same God who is bigger than the universe is also within each part of it. Yes, "in him we live and move and have our being" (Acts 17:28), but He also lives in us (in a very special way through the grace of Baptism) and acts in us.

St. Augustine had lots of struggles with family, friends, and romance when he was growing up, and he called God "higher than my highest thing and more inside than my most inside thing."[1]

God is not only the center of the big circle of love, He has to be the center of every one of the circles. Christ is not only the best friend we'll ever have, He's the most powerful one, too, and more than ready to lend *His* strength, *His* smarts, and *His* purity when we feel ours is lacking.

To live and grow in all of these circles, we all have to strive to be strong, smart, and pure, and we will get there only by working closely with God above us and within us. God's plan for you is to be a gift of love.

Discussion Questions

Answer and discuss these questions with your Dad.

1. What kind of friend are you? What qualities make you a good friend?

_____

_____

_____

2. Have you ever reached out in friendship to someone who was very different than you? What was the result?

_____

_____

_____

3. Do you have some friends who are girls? If so, why do you enjoy their company?

_____

_____

_____

4. Is there a particular girl you like better than all the others? How do you act around her?

_____

_____

_____

5. What are some concrete ways you can begin to develop your spiritual muscles (virtues)? Which one will you work on first?

_____

_____

_____

6. Have you ever prayed to God about your future vocation? What are some of the ideas that come to your mind about your future?

_____

_____

_____

7. What does it mean to be a gift of yourself to:

Family

_____

_____

_____

Friends

_____

_____

_____

God

_____

_____

_____

Chapter Reflections

While discussing this chapter, my Dad gave me some extra advice about . . .

_____

_____

_____

While reading this chapter, I learned these two important things:

1. _____

2. _____

I resolve to live out the *LoveEd* teachings from this chapter by . . .

_____

_____

_____

Finish this chapter with the following prayer:

Jesus, You made me to be a virtuous person, but it is not always easy for me. Open my eyes to the good around me so that I can make one good decision at a time and learn to love my family and friends with Your pure love. Help me to be a leader among my friends and a good example for all. Amen.

My Dad and I completed this chapter on

_____

(date and time)

CHAPTER 3

God's Supernatural Plan

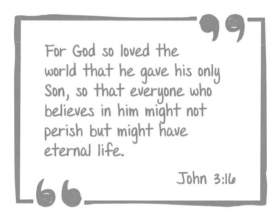

> For God so loved the world that he gave his only Son, so that everyone who believes in him might not perish but might have eternal life.
>
> John 3:16

The boy from the video, Michael, has a pretty cool name. He shares it with the chief archangel. If you happen to know a boy with the Spanish name *Miguelángel* (because that's more common these days than knowing an Italian kid—a dynamite in art class!—named Michelangelo), his name means "the angel Michael." But the name isn't Spanish or English or Italian. It's Hebrew, and it's about the best comeback ever.

According to an ancient tradition, the rebellious angel Lucifer was puffed up with pride and thought himself to be like God, meaning that he was practically in God's league. Michael, defending God's total awesomeness, challenged him, saying, "Who is like God?" (Roughly translated, "Are you kidding me? God is infinitely more than you, me, anyone, or anything!") In fact, the name *Michael* means "who is like God."

God created things to share in His glory, not to compete with Him for it. Our happiness consists in being who we are, not in trying to be greater (or lesser) than who we are. The Devil forgot that, and Michael reminded him. The Devil never ceases trying to get us to go along with his scheme. What did he promise Adam and Eve if they eat the forbidden fruit? "You will be like gods" (Gn 3:5). Same old mistake Michael smacked him down for.

But the question "Who is like God?" makes us think about two related and important questions: "Who is God?" and "What is God like?" How can we know, since we can't see Him? True, we don't see Him, but we see His works. We also believe that He Himself came down to show us what He is like. Let's look at both of these ways God reveals Himself to us.

The Works of God Teach Us about God

You haven't met Van Gogh. Nobody currently alive has. But we can learn a lot about him from his paintings. We can see his love of color, his passion in the curls and twists of his lines, and the huge amount of paint he put on the canvas. We know he liked sunflowers because he painted them often.

We know a lot more about Van Gogh because he painted himself. His dozens of self-portraits tell us that he saw himself as somewhat sad and serious. We know that he cut off his ear because he painted a few portraits with a bandaged ear, and every portrait after that shows his face from the side that still has an ear. We know his hair was blonde and that his beard, when he had one, was reddish.

We actually know a fair bit about a man we have never met. We also know quite a bit about a God we've never seen.

Before anything existed . . . there was God.

Always and everywhere, God is love. And in His great goodness, God had a plan to share His love by creating the universe and everything in it. And when He made the world, He made everything according to a grand design.

We see God's works. We know the order of the universe points to an intelligent Creator. And in these works we see power, beauty, subtlety, and amazing precision. The wiring in a butterfly's brain baffles the most knowledgeable computer circuit expert. Therefore, God as the source of power and beauty and wonder of nature must be supremely powerful and wondrous and beautiful as well.

Stars that glisten at night. Mountains that soar up to heaven and send water falling down to earth. Trees that stand beautiful in their solitude and majestic in their unity. Every single thing on earth God made to be perfect in itself.

When God made us, though, he did something extra. God made us in His own image. We are God's greatest idea, His artistic masterpiece: our bodies, our souls, our hearts, our minds. And since God created the human person in His own image, we are made for love. Our whole purpose for being is to love God and to love one another.

In fact, we know more about God when we look at ourselves than when we look at any other creature. And the reason is because we are made in God's image. We are His self-portrait! The invisible aspect of our nature, our soul that knows and loves, reveals to us a God of surpassing knowledge and love.

God gives every human being two great gifts that make us capable of loving: the ability to know and understand and the power to make free choices. We call those gifts our intellect and our free will.

But God is always, has always, and will always be knowing and loving. Before there was something else to know and love, He was knowing and loving . . . Himself! (But not in a weird way, the way narcissists are in love with themselves.)

This is a pretty big mystery, but God came down and revealed a bit of it to us through Jesus, His Son. Jesus Christ spoke of God as Father, Son, and Holy Spirit—three Persons in one God. We call this the Blessed Trinity.

St. John Paul II explained, "It has been said, in a beautiful and profound way, that our God in his deepest mystery is not a solitude, but a family, since he has in himself fatherhood, sonship and the essence of the family, which is love."[2]

So it is in His *works* that we see God's power and beauty and the amazing variety of His creativity (to make both blue whales and microorganisms like plankton shows some major range!). And it is in the *human person* that we see God's perfection of knowing and loving. But knowing and loving cannot happen in just one person alone. God created badgers and boll weevils and scorpions and everything else and then created man as the crowning achievement of His creative work. Every evening of the first five days of creation God said, "It is good." But then He said something wasn't good: "It is *not good* for the man to be alone" (Gn 2:18, emphasis added). One person alone is not a full enough self-portrait of God. God intended us to be a set, and that's why "male and female he created them" (Gn 1:27). We are made for community. We are made to live in a community of persons.

The reason for this is that, since God is "Father, Son, and Holy Spirit," a Community of Divine Persons, *only a community of persons shows who God is*. God's most important work is the human family, the community of persons formed by Adam and his wife, Eve. God gave the earth to them saying, "Be fertile and multiply; fill the earth and subdue it" (Gn 1:28).

The reason Van Gogh painted was to express himself. It was to show who he was on the inside. It's the same for every painter. And God creates to show who He is, to share His goodness, to bring all things toward the fulfillment He planned. A coach makes a game plan in order to win the game, but the victory is also for the players. After winning the Super Bowl, the players hand the trophy to the coach, but everyone is jumping for joy, and they all share in the victory.

But a team only wins if they follow the game plan. We will only share God's glory if we follow His plan. Just as you wouldn't vandalize a Van Gogh painting because you'd be destroying something valuable and insulting the artist who worked hard to express himself, we should never knowingly violate God's plan, because it destroys something valuable and offends God who, with this plan, is showing the world who He is.

Although it sounds impossible, when it comes to the family, there is something more at stake here than heaven and hell. We have been entrusted with delivering a message to the world. This message is *who God is*, what His love is like. If we fail to live up to that, we have fumbled our lives away. Game over.

The World's Worst Fumble and Greatest Recovery

However, right from the beginning the human race failed to follow God's plan. We chose our own will rather than God's. That is the reality we call sin. Sin goes against the beauty and order of God's creation. Adam and Eve gave in to the Devil's temptation and his false promise "to be like gods" and disobeyed the one commandment God asked them to keep. They were led to see God not as the source of their fulfillment, not the coach that would lead them to victory, but as their rival who was keeping them down. This was the biggest lie in the history of mankind. Thus, they failed to execute the game plan and fumbled big time.

Sin can be found in each of the three love circles. Our unloving choices have negative consequences for ourselves and for those whose lives touch ours. Sin tears families apart, ruins friendships, and corrupts romantic relationships.

Adam and Eve even turned and blamed each other. The first family was breaking apart. But God right then and there promised a Redeemer who would come to crush the head of the serpent (see Gn 3:15). The family is deeply involved with victory over evil. Every family lives out a battle for love, and God wants us to emerge victorious.

But here's the rest of the story.

God never stops loving us. When we sin, God always gives us another chance to come home to Him and ask for forgiveness. Jesus died for our sins. Jesus is God Himself, God the Son, who came down to show us what God is like, what love is like. Jesus reminded us of the importance of the family and of God's original plan in creating us male and female. And when we are wounded by another person's sin, God sends someone to bring us the healing power of His love. God's love is always greater than our sin. This is the amazing good news that Jesus came to earth to show us: God's love is always greater than our sin. God's love is greater even than death.

Our loving God is still present in our world. God is with us now, every day, in all of our love circles.

Jesus also earned special power for us: a sharing in God's own life and power that we call grace. So the biggest fumble ever led to the biggest recovery ever. Adam and Eve got kicked out of the Garden of Eden. Jesus came and opened not Eden for us but heaven itself. Through Christ's grace we become adopted sons and daughters of the royal family of the universe! In a sense, we are way better off than Adam and Eve ever were. They were destined to live forever on earth. We have a shot at living with God in heaven!

So we should be faithful to God's plan because, to

earn that grace, Jesus had to die for us. We live faithfully as a thank you to our Creator but also to our Redeemer—to Jesus, who took a bullet for us, a bullet that involved the horrible torture of the Cross.

Christ the Bridegroom

When St. Paul speaks about marriage, he says it is a great mystery that has to do with Christ and His Church. Jesus shows that God's love for us all (in the human community He came to save, His Church) is like a husband's love for his bride. The Church is often called the "Bride of Christ." And the bridegroom gives his all for his bride, his entire self. Jesus gave His whole life. Your Dad and Mom give their lives to each other each day. As a young man, you are preparing yourself to give your all for others.

Marriage is not only a natural institution but among baptized persons, it is a sacrament, a visible sign of invisible grace. Marriage is a way in which God's grace comes into the world, and the ministers of this grace of marriage are not the bishops or priests but married people themselves. At a Catholic wedding, the priest witnesses the marriage on behalf of the Church, but the man and woman getting married are themselves the ministers! (That's one of the great Catholic trivia questions, by the way. Ask people: "What is the only sacrament the pope cannot administer?" It will drive them crazy. The answer is marriage, because the ministers of that sacrament are the spouses. Any priest, even the pope himself, may celebrate the wedding Mass and administer the Eucharist, but when it comes to the marriage itself, he is a witness and not a minister.)

Jesus's death on the Cross shows us who God is. He is love, the total gift of self.

As God's self-portraits and especially as His adopted children, we are fulfilled by imitating this total gift of self. This can be done in two ways.

First, we can give ourselves to God directly in a total gift of self to the community. This is done by consecrating ourselves to God in the priesthood, religious life, or consecrated single life. The reason that consecrated souls don't get married is not because they hate marriage or couldn't find anyone who would marry them. They respect what marriage means, but they hear a call from God to a different vocation. It is a sacrifice for them to give up marriage and family life. They make that sacrifice to give themselves to God totally in their self-giving to all of us.

The other and most common way of giving ourselves to God totally is through the gift of ourselves to another person. *One* other person. This is God's plan for marriage.

You can only give yourself totally to God directly or to one other person. There is no other way. Anything else is not a total gift of self and is not following Jesus's example or the model of the Trinity.

God's Playbook for Body and Soul

Each of us is a unity of body and soul. We are not our bodies alone, and we are not our souls alone. So the body is part of our gift of self; it becomes a sharer in spiritual love. Love includes the human body.

Every level of human relationship has physical expressions. You got bounced on your dad's lap when you were younger, you high-five your friends or whack them on the shoulder after a great play. You give your mom a kiss good night. These are all "body language" ways of saying, "You're important to me; I want to be a part of your life."

But none of these ways express a total gift of self. A total gift of self says, "I give myself to you and only you. Forever." We call this kind of promise a wedding vow.

You have to be strong to give a total gift of self. You have to be smart, since you have to know all about yourself to know what all you have to give. And you have to be pure, because the gift has to be pure you. You can't give something else and pawn it off as you. That's being a fake and a fraud.

There are plenty of fakes and frauds out there. In the 1960s, people started talking about a "sexual revolution" where sex would be finally free from what they called the chains of morality and religion. The sad thing is that, when used in any way other than to express a total gift of self, sex leads to sadness and frustration, even if there are fleeting moments of physical pleasure.

Impurity leads to a life that is ultimately a failure because we can only be fulfilled in a true and total gift of self. That's why sex outside of marriage is so wrong. God wants only the best for us, so He gives us the Church to guide us and help us live our best life.

If you wanted to buy the best BMX bike on the market and had been saving up for months, you would have to save all of your money, your *total* savings. If you kept spending it on other things, you would never have enough for the bike you really want. You would not be purely saving, but saving "impurely."

It's the same with our gift of self.

And you know why, don't you? When our gift is lame, we're throwing away the grace Christ earned for us on the Cross. When our gift is shabby, we don't reflect the love God put into our creation. When our gift is not a gift at all but rather something self-centered, we do not execute the playbook God wrote for us. Our lives will not share in God's victory. Hell is a real possibility.

God's plan is amazing. It's perfect. His playbook is *guaranteed* to work, since He is all-wise and all-powerful. But He made us free. He isn't going to run onto the field and carry the ball when He made us perfectly capable of doing so. We have to execute. We have to trust that His plan is the one that will work and not pay attention to anyone coming with any bright ideas that contradict God's plan.

"Coach is calling for a sweep left. On two." Who in the huddle is going to say, "Well, I think we should go off-tackle left. Um . . . on one"? Someone who won't be on the team long enough to enjoy the championship, that's for sure.

God's plan in nature works hand-in-hand with His supernatural plan. For Jesus to die for us, He had to become man and grow up and give Himself totally for us in His death on the Cross.

You're changing and becoming a man. Your body is growing strong so you can become the father of a family and protect your wife and children. You're learning things so you can be wise and guide them to truth and provide for them with your physical and intellectual work. Your body is also changing so you can give the total gift of self that will bond you to your future wife and create a family of your own.

You are a gift that God put on this earth. You were a gift for your parents and your siblings. And now you're getting ready to give that gift to someone else and in this way give yourself back to God in your dedication to a new family. Being strong, smart, and pure is the way to do that.

Your teen years and your time as a young man are your training camp. You'll be learning the playbook that is God's plan for your life, especially His plan for marriage. You'll be hitting the tackling dummies and blocking sleds, forming the habits of virtue that are needed for you to be victorious. And you'll be spending time with your coach so you can grow in confidence, knowing that this is the man who will lead you to a championship. You will also learn to recognize your opponents' plays and how they will try to defeat you.

If you strive to form the habits of self-giving and virtue, you will strengthen all of your circles. Bad choices strain and break families, destroy friendships, and pervert romantic relationships. Habits of virtue unite families, create long-lasting friendships, and spark relationships that can mature into faithful marriages and strong new families. So wake up each day looking for a fight—what St. Paul called the "good fight" of faith (see 1 Tm 6:12).

The Christian life is a battle each day. Giving yourself to God and others is a daily struggle. But God made you tough, and God's grace will make you a hero.

Discussion Questions

Answer and discuss these questions with your Dad.

1. What is the most beautiful place you have seen in nature? What did you like most about it?

_____

_____

_____

2. Describe a way your parents have helped you learn about God.

_____

_____

_____

3. How often do you go to confession? Discuss with your
   Dad what each of you knows about God's unconditional
   mercy and love.

_____

_____

_____

4. God has given us free will. How can you train your
   will to choose what is good in an area where you are
   struggling now?

_____

_____

_____

5. What does it mean to be a "total gift of self"? How does
   that compare with a fake or partial gift? Look back into
   this chapter or chapter two if you need some ideas; this
   is a HUGE question to think about over and over again
   in life, so let's start now.

_____

_____

_____

Chapter Reflections

While discussing this chapter, my Dad gave me some extra advice about . . .

_____

_____

_____

While reading this chapter, I learned these two important things:

1. _____

2. _____

I resolve to live out the *LoveEd* teachings from this chapter by . . .

_____

_____

_____

Finish this chapter with the following prayer:

Thank You for giving meaning to my life. Thank You for making me in your image and likeness. Give me the grace, O God, to serve You always. Help me to avoid offending You so that I can have the life of abundance that You designed for me. Amen.

My Dad and I completed this chapter on

_____

(date and time)

CHAPTER 4

God's Plan for Natural Changes

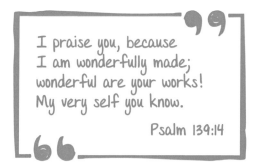

I praise you, because
I am wonderfully made;
wonderful are your works!
My very self you know.

Psalm 139:14

When we profess our faith by reciting the Creed on Sunday, the first thing we say is "I believe in one God, the Father almighty, maker of heaven and earth, of all things visible and invisible." We profess our faith in God who made everything we see and things we cannot see. The natural order was created by God. It is called the natural *order* because there is an order to it. This order itself points to a Creator. Dominoes don't get lined up by random chance. When we respect the order that exists within creation, we are respecting and obeying God's plan. Following God's plan is what gives us fulfillment and victory in life.

One of the things that most characterizes the natural world is change. It is change that scientists study, measure, and categorize. They try to figure out the laws that govern all the changes. You have noticed changes happening in and around you. There's a fair amount of science about them. Science discovers and reveals God's plan in nature.

God made boys to be different than girls. He created human beings as two different sexes: male and female. Men and women were designed to "complement" each other, not "compete" with one another. They were created to work together, not fight against one another. What if a men's football team played against a women's football team? Okay, you know who would probably win. Is it because boys are better? Well, maybe at football, but not at everything! God gave men different gifts than he gave women, and one of His gifts to men is greater physical strength. It is not fair for women and men to compete with one another when it comes to physical strength—but when it comes to competing in the spelling bee, that's a different story. Study on!

Man and woman . . . male and female . . . what is this all for? God had a plan from the beginning, from the very creation of man, to have men and women made for love, marriage, and giving life! God made male and female bodies so they complement and complete one another while reflecting His love to the world.

In marriage, a man and woman work together to care for their family the best way they can. Like a football player, the man might be out at work crashing into the problems of the world and avoiding obstacles as he tries to get his team to the goal. He trains, practices, and educates himself to be the best husband, dad, and provider he can be. That is also true for the father of a family when he tries every strategy and practice to deliver his family, "his team," to heaven. A man's wife, as his partner and helpmate, works alongside him building their family, at work, in the home, or out in the world. Both husband and wife should encourage each other and motivate the other to reach the "goal" as they live out the great virtues they want their children to possess. In a way, parents are "coaches" for virtue. When a man becomes a priest, his attempt to reach the goal is similar. He gives his whole self toward getting his team—his parishioners and/or students—to heaven.

Did you ever realize that a father's job is to lead his family to heaven? God wants your parents to teach you this information about the goodness of growing up. God and your parents want you to grow into a good man who is on his way to heaven. They want you to be happy here on earth and happy for all of eternity.

Each person is born as either a male or a female baby. The male baby grows to become a boy that eventually develops into a man. The female baby grows to become a girl that later in life matures into a woman. The image and dignity of God is given to both wonderfully created sexes.

God created your body to work in fascinating ways. Imagine how all the systems of your body are working inside of you so you can see, hear, digest your food, eliminate waste, circulate your blood, and breathe. The human body is truly amazing! Many of these things take place, not because you choose for them to happen, but because God set them in motion when He created our first parents.

God wants us to know the truth about the beautiful way He made our bodies, a way that reflects His beauty and love. God made us to love and serve Him by offering other people His life-giving love. We love others with the thoughts of our minds, the love of our hearts, and through our daily actions. Being kind, caring, and generous to everyone are a few of the ways we can share God's love with the world.

Without realizing it, we are always growing and changing. God designed both our bodies and our souls to reflect his love. As we grow up, we mature in many ways that are both spiritual and physical. God wants us to know the truth about our souls and our bodies and how and why they grow.

God designed each person with many automatic control centers called glands. There is one gland in the brain that sends signals through our bloodstream to tell our body to grow. This gland is called the pituitary gland. When we're children, the pituitary gland sends growth hormones into our bloodstream that tell our bones, muscles, and other tissues to grow. A child's growth may depend on the rate that his or her parents grew and on the size they grew to be. Some people will be short and others will be tall; some will be stocky; some will be thin. People come in all shapes and sizes. Each person is unique and special to God.

Your body also changes shape as you grow. When you're five years old, you are not just a taller baby. You stand differently, and you have longer bones and less of a belly. Your head is in a different proportion to your torso and legs as well. The same is true for adulthood. You're not just a "bigger child." Your body undergoes physical changes as it matures into adulthood.

From the beginning of life, all the body systems except

one are fully working. The
exception is the reproductive system, which is uniquely
programmed to mature later
when we're in our preteens or
teens. There is a particular time
of growth called puberty, when a
boy grows into a man and a girl

grows into a woman. Puberty is the beginning of what
we call adolescence. During adolescence while our bodies are growing, our souls are also meant to grow in love
and grace so we will better reflect the image of God in our
hearts, minds, and wills. It's up to us to work with the help
of God's grace to grow in virtue and love so we will be spiritually, mentally, and socially mature when we become fully
physically mature.

Puberty is a time for boys to start to become examples
of kindness, protectors of life, and leaders for goodness,
much like St. Joseph. Girls must also begin to initiate a sincere concern for goodness, become examples of virtue and
warmth, and develop a strong self-image and character in
imitation of the Blessed Virgin Mary. As we said earlier, we
are all called to be strong, smart, and pure.

Puberty: What's it all about?

The time of puberty usually lasts about four years. For boys,
puberty usually occurs between the ages of eleven and sev-
enteen, with the average age being fourteen years old. For
girls, the average age to reach puberty is thirteen, but anytime between the ages of nine and sixteen is considered
normal. Puberty is a time for the body to grow bigger, not
just in height and weight, but also to mature into adulthood

so that a person is prepared to possibly become a parent when he or she is married. This is why, at puberty, the pituitary gland sends out another type of hormone, a maturing hormone.

What happens at puberty? A girl's body begins to change into a woman's body, and a boy's body begins to change into a man's body. During puberty and adolescence, a person's thoughts and emotions change as well. It might seem confusing at first, but the new changes will become more balanced as you grow over the next few years. Just as it takes time to learn how to walk and how to talk, it takes time to grow into a woman or a man. It also takes time to understand how marvelously God has created the human body and why He has designed us the way He has.

How does puberty happen? God has programmed the changes to take place during the preteen and teen years through the hormones and tissues in your endocrine and reproductive system.

What should I do about puberty? For the physical changes, you need to take care of your body by eating the right foods, getting enough sleep, and keeping your body safe and clean. When you experience emotional changes such as confusion, irritability, anger, sadness, and other feelings, you can practice self-control over your words and actions, no matter what your moods or emotions are. As we will see in chapter five, when you experience spiritual changes, whether they're deeper thoughts or new temptations, you'll want to stay close to God by growing in your prayer life and by receiving God's graces by frequent participation in the sacraments.

What happens to my body first when I reach puberty?
There are hormone changes and body growth spurts that sometimes increase body odor and perspiration while the sweat glands mature. When these changes occur, an underarm deodorant is used daily to stop the odor or to keep it from being noticed by others. Don't wait for your brothers and sisters to tell you that you smell! Pay attention at this age, and when your parents tell you to take a shower, just take one. You'll need to shower more often now than you did when you were a child.

Sometime between the ages of eleven and fifteen, a hormone in your bloodstream called testosterone will begin to increase. Testosterone has always been in your body, but now you might notice its effects in a more obvious way.

At the moment God created you in your mother's womb, He programmed into your tiny system that you would be a boy and that you would grow the organs and body type of a boy. Testosterone is present in boys even before birth. Some research shows that a male baby's brain is different from a female baby's brain even when still in the womb. This difference happens when testosterone crosses the blood-brain barrier and "masculinizes" the brain. There is more to being a boy or being a girl than we can even see.

As boy babies grow, the testosterone in their bodies helps increase muscle mass and bone density. This process is not as intense for baby girls. God prepared you to be strong from the beginning of your life.

Now, at puberty, there are more visible effects of the quickly rising testosterone levels in your bloodstream. These effects might be an adult type of body odor, increased oiliness of skin and hair, and maybe even acne. You will begin to grow faster, which we call a "growth spurt" when your bones become even longer and thicker. Hair will grow in new places, such as in your armpits and pubic area. And, as every man knows, the fine hairs on your face will become darker and thicker on your upper lip, chin, and sideburns so that a mustache and a beard become possible choices. Chest hair may start growing as well. Arm hair, leg hair— hey, depending on the genes of your ancestors, you might notice hair growing in all sorts of places on your body!

Your body shape will begin to change, too. As your bones grow longer, your shoulders will become broader, and your rib cage will expand. Muscle mass and strength will increase. Your nose, jaw, brow, chin, and facial bones will all be divinely remodeled as you change from looking like a boy to looking like a man. This stage in life might feel a little awkward. You may grow so fast that you bump into doorways or trip as you adjust to your new size. Relax. This growth has happened to every man so far. It is all part of growing up, and eventually you will be comfortable in your new body.

Eventually, one of life's more embarrassing moments will take place: Your voice changes! That unisex voice from boyhood starts to deepen and sound more like a man. The change happens gradually. One day your voice might even squeak, crack, and change while you're talking. Don't be embarrassed! It's time to thank God that you are becoming a man. It would be worse if you remained a boy all your life, wouldn't it? You may notice that your Adam's apple, which is the voice box you can see behind the skin on your neck, will begin to be more prominent.

Those might be the changes you notice on the outside of your body at puberty, but that's not all that is changing. There is also physical maturity taking place on the inside of your body. The reproductive organs—penis, testicles, and scrotum—will grow and change as well. The penis is the male sex organ that provides for the release of urine and semen to the outside of the body. The testicles are two ball-shaped organs in a male that produce hormones and the reproductive cells called sperm cells. The scrotum is the soft pouch of skin on the outside of the body between a man's legs that contain the two testes (testicles). The testes are the main organs that release the large amounts of the male hormone, testosterone, into your blood stream that causes all these changes in you at puberty. These are called the genital organs because they help generate life.

Testosterone signals your testes to create sperm cells, the reproductive cells needed for you to become a father someday. As the testosterone levels rise in your blood-stream, you may experience some feelings of sexual urges that come with an attraction to women. The same girls you didn't notice a few years ago suddenly begin to look different in your eyes. You may experience feelings of attraction that you did not have when you were younger. Sometimes the urges might come in the middle of the night, even if you were not thinking about girls. On occasion, sperm cells, mixed with fluid called semen, might come out of your penis while you are asleep. This is called a wet dream or, more formally, a nocturnal emission, and it is one way God prepares your body to have children when you are married. This occurs naturally and is no cause for worry. Wet dreams occur less often as boys move through puberty, and they eventually stop.

It seems like a lot is going on in your body in a few short

years, but this is all part of God's plan of growing from a boy into a man. Testosterone affects your entire body, oftentimes enlarging your heart, lungs, and liver so they can serve your new man-sized body, too.

A young man may also experience an erection. This is a hardening of the penis due to an increase of blood flow in that area. An erection can happen due to stress, excitement, or boredom; it can occur during sleep, upon waking, or for no reason at all. It is normal for erections to happen to boys at puberty, but erections also can happen to boys of any age. If ignored, the erection will go away on its own. It is wrong for a boy to rub or stimulate himself to cause or to prolong an erection. If a young man does nothing to cause the erection, there is no sin. Similarly, if a young man is tempted to entertain impure thoughts or actions and resists those thoughts, there is no sin either. A young man can train his mind to say a quick prayer and think of other things that are good and wholesome. If erections are experienced often due to boredom or stress, try some good ways to release built up energy or tension. These would include daily exercise, more active sports games, and keeping busy and active doing good deeds for other people. The good old-fashioned cold shower can also help.

What other changes occur during puberty? You can expect to experience some mental or psychological changes during the teen years, too. You might start thinking more deeply about the meaning of things than you did when you were a child. Your mind might start to see things in a more complicated manner. Feelings of independence and a desire to do things differently than your parents may arise as well. You may feel more tempted to disobey or disrespect your parents. It's important to practice resisting any temptations to disobey or rebel so you can practice glorifying God with all of your choices. Imitate Jesus, who as an adolescent and teen, loved, respected, and obeyed Mary and St. Joseph completely (see Lk 2:51).

During adolescence, you may experience new, unfamiliar emotions. Romantic feelings and feelings of attraction are sure to come up. Emotions and feelings are normal; it is how you behave that is important. The feelings themselves are neither morally good nor bad. What matters is how you choose to speak, think, act, and treat people when you have these feelings. Romantic feelings can make you happy and help you become less selfish, but these feelings do not have to be acted upon by trying to get the attention of the opposite sex. Other feelings, like those of sadness or crankiness, can drag you down if you let them. Instead try to find ways to care for others that help cheer you up.

The changes experienced in adolescence are all part of a good process, a process designed by God to help you mature. It's up to you to make the choice to behave virtuously when faced with these new feelings. When you make the right choices, you will grow in maturity and inner strength. The virtues of self-control, modesty, purity, and chastity are important virtues to develop during this time. Remember that a virtue is a habit of doing good, so take the frequent opportunities presented by life to build up your inner strength, one good choice at a time.

Other changes occur that are sometimes difficult to explain or deal with. There may be sudden mood changes (due to the hormone changes), self-consciousness (thinking everybody is watching you), desires for more freedom and decision-making (which you should discuss with your parents), more understanding of yourself, and a concern for helping others rather than just focusing on yourself. These signs of maturity may come and go during the adolescent years. Practicing mature and virtuous behavior, no matter how you're feeling, can help you complete your personal maturity process and become a true leader for goodness and virtue.

But along with *what* is happening, there is a deeper question: *why?*

Why does puberty happen? God created puberty so that, after you are married, you could bring new life into the world. It's amazing that God has so perfectly designed our bodies that we can actually cocreate life with Him! Having children is God's plan for marriage. God made us out of love to love and to be loved. Man and woman are to reflect His creative love to the world as husband and wife within the sacrament of Marriage.

A very simple answer is that without the union of the adult male and female persons, the human race could not continue. The basic answer to the question "Where do babies come from?" is "From a man and a woman." It's worth repeating in today's confused world: One man and one woman, united in married love, can create a wonderful and beautiful family. We see that God's "invisible" plan of love and attraction can be revealed when a man and a woman make God's love "visible" through married love that brings new life. The couple's love comes alive in a whole new person—their baby!

God made men and women to be different yet complementary, meaning that they are opposite but made to go together. Their bodies reflect this "complementarity." Men and women are equal in dignity, yet they are different in the way they think and act. God designed each sex, male and female, to have a different role in creating new life, and *each* is required to create this new life. Let's take a look at what goes on inside a man and a woman that gives them the power to cocreate new human life with God.

At puberty, when a boy becomes a man and a girl becomes a woman, one of the systems in the body—the reproductive system—develops in such a way that the man and woman become capable of joining together to create a new human life. This ability to create new life with God is called their fertility. Fertility is both a gift from God and a gift to each other. In the Book of Genesis, God commanded Adam and Eve to "be fertile and multiply, fill the earth and subdue it" (Gn 1:28), meaning they should use the gift their fertility to bring new life into the world.

What goes on inside a woman that makes her able to conceive and nurture a new human life? Young women are the future mothers of the world. God has given women hearts with strong emotions that can love deeply and overcome hardships. He gave young women beautiful bodies that are naturally attractive to men so that men can see the beauty of God through them.

The first changes that occur during puberty for a girl are the development of her breasts. A woman's breasts are designed by God to produce human milk, the perfect food for a new baby. Inside the breast are mammary glands, ducts that produce milk soon after a baby is born. As the baby nurses from the mother, the breast begins to produce more milk. This is all programmed by God to take place based on the baby's needs after he or she is born.

The woman's reproductive organs are hidden safely

inside her lower abdomen. They are called the genitals, because God designed them to generate life. Her main organs are the ovaries, the uterus, the vagina, and the fallopian tubes. The ovaries produce hormones and egg cells, and the fallopian tubes connect the ovaries to the uterus. The uterus is often called the womb. The womb is a sacred space where God creates new life. The vagina is the passageway from the uterus to the outside of the woman's body. It also serves as the birth canal as a baby leaves the womb to enter the outside world.

From the time of puberty in a young woman, one egg cell matures each month until the time of menopause, when a woman is about fifty years old. A woman's egg cell contains half of the genetic material needed to conceive a new baby. During the time of each month while the egg is maturing in the ovary, the uterus is preparing for the possibility of cradling a new life. The lining of the uterus thickens with blood to make it able to nourish a new baby. When the egg cell is released, it travels from the ovary through the Fallopian tube toward the uterus. God has programmed this to happen naturally. If the egg cell is fertilized by the male sperm cell during the marriage act, a baby will begin to grow and nestle itself in the thick nourishing lining of the mother's uterus. If the egg cell is not fertilized by the male sperm cell, it passes into the uterus and dissolves. If there is no baby starting to grow, the blood-filled lining of the uterus is not needed, so it is released at the end of the month to the outside of the body through the vagina. This releasing of the excess lining is a monthly process called menstruation, or a woman's period. A woman will not have her period the whole nine months she is pregnant. Her body will be busy nourishing the baby inside her womb.

The Creation of New Life

Earlier, we spoke of the changes a man's body undergoes during puberty and how he experiences the beginnings of attraction and the sexual drive. The sexual drive is a power that should be used to glorify God at the service of His love. It's wrong to use these sexual powers for selfish pleasure or mere entertainment. This sexual drive, along with sexual pleasure, gives men and women the motivation and desire to carry on the human race and bond to one another in a loving relationship for life. These desires are good and not evil, though people can choose good or evil actions when they have those desires. The feelings of attraction, as well as all feelings, can and should be managed according to what is right and good. The more we practice controlling our behavior and turning our thoughts toward God when we have sexual feelings, the greater will be our emotional maturity and sexual self-mastery. God has a plan for these intimate feelings to become part of the bonding process of husband and wife in a lifelong marriage.

At the wedding ceremony, the couple promises before God that they will be open to having the children God wants them to have. After they're married, during the conjugal union called sexual intercourse, the sperm cells from the husband travel into the vagina of his wife. If an egg cell is present in the woman, a new human life, made in the image of God, is formed at the moment a sperm cell from the man joins together with the egg cell of the woman. This is the moment when God, with the cooperation of the man and woman, creates an entirely unique and unrepeatable person: body *and* soul. Married love and the conjugal union were designed for this very moment—to generate new life out of love. The act of sexual intercourse is naturally designed to take place only between members of the opposite sex—one man and one woman—through the joining of their genital organs in a loving marital embrace. This is why it is also called the marriage, or marital, act.

When the unique genetic traits carried in a single sperm cell from the man merge with the unique traits of that month's one-of-a-kind egg cell of the woman, the life of a new child is set in motion by God's plan. This moment when new life begins is called conception.

Although God requires the cooperation of the man and woman for conception to occur, His almighty power takes over from that point on. God has programmed life to rapidly grow at the time the two cells forge as one. At conception, the baby has all the genetic information it needs to become the boy or girl it is intended to be. God has prepared the woman's body to receive and nurture this new human life, their baby. He has chosen this one sperm cell, out of the millions of others present in the father's semen, to be the one cell to unite with this one ovum from the mother. The unique qualities of this new person are known by God, and He sets the pace for growth. We know this because the Bible tells us, "Before I formed you in the womb I knew you" (Jer 1:5), and "You knit me in my mother's womb" (Ps 139:13). God chooses to create boys and girls whose souls will live for all eternity. The man and woman, father and mother, are privileged to participate in this cocreation of new life. This power to cocreate with God is called procreation.

At the moment of conception, the little child of God that is conceived is either a boy or a girl. The mother's egg cell carries the X chromosome, and the father's sperm cell carries either an X or Y chromosome. The sex of the baby is determined depending on whether the father's sperm cell that penetrated the mother's egg cell carries the X or Y chromosome. The joining of an X and X becomes a girl, and the joining of an X and Y becomes a boy. The DNA present in the cells creates the new baby's unique genetic identity receiving the physical and mental traits of the parents and grandparents, showing God's intricate plan in the design of the human body. You are "wonderfully made" (Ps 139:14). This tiny new life even produces its own hormones to keep the mother's body from rejecting it. According to God's natural plan, the baby will continue to grow in the mother's womb for nine months of pregnancy before being delivered to the outside world at birth.

The tiny baby is a unique human being from the moment of conception and gradually grows for nine months in the mother's womb. A mother is responsible for taking care of her health during this time by eating well, getting enough rest and exercise, and avoiding harmful habits.

The baby grows slowly through various stages as programmed by God during these nine months. In the first stage, the baby is called an embryo. After conception, the tiny baby continues to travel down the mother's fallopian tube to implant itself in the lining of the uterus and develop an umbilical cord and placenta that attaches to the inside of the uterus. The umbilical cord is the lifeline of nourishment for the baby that connects to the mother's blood stream by way of the uterine wall. Within eighteen days of conception, the baby's tiny heart is growing and beating; the mother may not even know she is pregnant yet. The mother usually discovers she is pregnant when she misses her next menstrual period.

At six to seven weeks old, the baby is about one inch long and his or her heart waves can be detected. The tiny skeleton is complete, while the arms, legs, body, and face are taking a more definite shape. At approximately twelve weeks old, the baby is more than three inches long. It is now called a fetus. Fingernails and toes appear, the arms and legs can move, and the baby can suck its thumb and do a somersault inside the mother's uterus.

During the fourth to sixth months of pregnancy, the baby grows to about eight to twelve inches long and weighs one to two pounds. The baby can now hear sounds, such as its mother's heartbeat, and can even recognize voices of familiar people. The mother can now feel the baby moving inside of her.

A full term baby is born about thirty-eight to forty weeks after conception. The birth process begins when the uterus muscles contract and start to push the baby down through the birth canal and out into the world for his or her first breath. He or she will no longer need the umbilical cord for nourishment, so the cord is disconnected at birth. God provides all the nourishment that the baby needs right after birth through the mother's breast milk. The baby is born with an instinct to suckle the breast to receive and swallow the milk that is produced by the mother's mammary glands.

The new child is ready for life outside of the womb with

its mother and father and will continue to grow if he or she receives proper love and nourishment. It's amazing to note that the baby can quickly recognize the difference between its mother and father and receives love from each of them in their unique masculine and feminine ways. The mother and father are responsible to God to continue to love and teach their child until he or she reaches adulthood.

It's natural for the mom and dad to love the cute and cuddly new baby born of their love. Babies are God's special gift to the couple and to the world.

Catholics Respect Life

Catholics respect and protect the dignity of each human life at every age, from conception until natural death. The science of conception and the miracle of life give us the understanding of why abortion is so evil and what it means to be pro-life. An abortion is the killing of an innocent baby while it still in the womb of the mother or removing the baby from the mother's womb during the pregnancy and leaving it to die.

This killing of an innocent baby is appalling to those of us who understand what is really happening in an abortion. An abortion kills the new baby who is a creation of God's love. You may hear people that are blind to this scientific truth about conception say, "It really isn't a baby," or "It's part of the mother's body, so it's the woman's right to choose." How confused these people must be to not realize that it is wrong to kill an innocent child of any size or age. It's as if they see the baby as something equivalent to the mother's arm (a "part of her") which she has the complete right to determine the fate of. But a baby is not like an arm; it is a human being. Abortion is always wrong. All Catholics should stand up for life in their thoughts, words, and actions.

Many Catholics work in the pro-life movement to help pregnant mothers who might be afraid that they cannot take care of their baby. Sometimes it's just the help they need to choose to continue the pregnancy and give life to the baby. Others in the pro-life movement work to change the current laws that allow abortion, and their efforts are just as important. In addition to all this, since an abortion can have long-term effects on the abortive mother's body, mind, and heart, most dioceses now also have retreats and counseling to help mothers heal from their past if they did choose to have an abortion. The Church is here to help and heal, and to respect all life.

Openness to Life

When a couple gets married, they promise during the wedding ceremony that they will "accept children lovingly from God." Catholics who know their science understand that a child is not conceived every time a couple participates in the marital union. There is a certain week of the month when the woman is fertile, and a man is usually fertile each day of the month. Catholic couples should learn and understand their monthly cycle of fertility so they can prayerfully and generously plan their family according to God's design for them. This is called Natural Family Planning, or NFP, as you might hear it called sometimes.

The Church teaches that God designed every conjugal act to be open to the possibility of life. We cannot, or should not, try to change the meaning of the marital act; it is the body language that means "total gift of self." In the spiritual and physical design of the marriage act, the love-giving cannot be separated from the life-giving, or the couple cheats themselves with only a "partial gift of self." If a married couple has a serious reason for spacing births, they may abstain from the marriage act during days of that month the woman is fertile, thus respecting the meaning of the marriage act. It is against God's plan for love and marriage if a couple tries to remove or block the life-giving from the conjugal act by using a contraceptive or any form of birth control. Your Dad's *Parent Guide* has more information about this topic if you want to ask him questions.

Even on the purely natural plane, the circle of romantic love we spoke of expands to a new family circle. The natural, visible level of love and life reveals some important things about God's plan in the invisible realm. We have seen that these miracles of life and love reveal that we, as God's creatures, are called to imitate Him in a total gift of self.

God's beautiful plan is just beginning to unfold in your body now, preparing you for the fulfilling future He desires for you.

Discussion Questions

Answer and discuss these questions with your Dad.

1. In your own words, describe God's design for sexuality and marriage. Why is it so important to understand and respect His design? How will it help you learn to love?

_____

_____

_____

2. How would you define real love?

_____

_____

_____

3. How is God's plan for marriage and family being challenged today by our culture? What do you see out there that contradicts His design for chastity, modesty and purity?

_____

_____

_____

4. What are some things you should do in order to lead a pure life? What are some things you should avoid? Think of what you see, say, hear, touch, and what thoughts enter your mind, and how each of those affects your purity.

_____

_____

_____

5. What would you say to a friend who says abortion is not wrong? How would you help him see the error of that stance?

_____

_____

_____

6. What are some virtues that a man will need in order to live out God's plan for marriage, which is both natural and supernatural? (Hint: re-check that list of virtues from Act 2.)

_____

_____

_____

Chapter Reflections

While discussing this chapter, my Dad gave me some extra advice about . . .

_____

_____

_____

While reading this chapter, I learned these two important things:

1. _____

2. _____

I resolve to live out the *LoveEd* teachings from this chapter by . . .

_____

_____

_____

Finish this chapter with the following prayer:

God, our Father, thank You for creating me in such a marvelous way. Thank You for the wisdom to use the knowledge You give me. Keep me in awe and reverence of the powers You have entrusted to me to love and to give life. Amen.

My Dad and I completed this chapter on

_____

(date and time)

CHAPTER 5

Your Answer to God's Plan

> Do you not know that the runners in the stadium all run in the race, but only one wins the prize? Run so as to win. Every athlete exercises discipline in every way. They do it to win a perishable crown, but we an imperishable one.
>
> 1 Corinthians 9:24–25

With so many changes, you may feel that your life is spinning in circles, but we have seen that those circles are all part of God's plan. He has a plan for your body and for your soul, and He has a plan for the salvation of the world; He wants to show the world the love that is at the very heart of the Trinity.

The game plan is all set. The playbook is written. It's game day.

The question now is: Are you going to follow your Coach's instructions? What are the habits and skills you need to follow God's plan for your life, especially His plan for love and family life?

A ballplayer needs good habits. There's no time in the game to think about what you're going to do, so the reactions have to become second nature. A running back doesn't pause and say, "I think I'll hit this hole hard and then juke that linebacker." He just does it. And he does it because he has formed the habit of doing it a thousand times in practice. Every coach repeats this, so you've probably heard it somewhere: "You'll play like you practice."

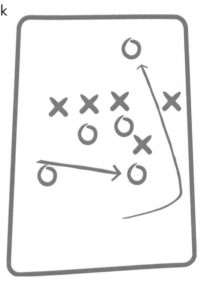

Habits in sports are mostly physical. Athletic training is training of the body. Moral growth is a training of the soul. While sports require you to move the right way and have the right motions (pitching mechanics or swing technique in baseball, ball control in soccer, etc.), moral growth requires you to make the right *choices*. It's all about developing habits of the will in order to choose the right things. We can define a virtue as a habit of the will to choose the right thing.

These habits of the will lead to other habits. By instinct, we move away from things that can harm or kill our bodies, like fire or an electric shock. By virtue, we train ourselves to recoil from sin, which can harm or kill our souls.

We don't get to choose what things are harmful or are good for us. We can't make fire harmless by wishing it so. The same is true in the moral order of things. What is good or harmful to us is already set in stone, so to speak. God took care of that when He made us. He knows what's good for us and what's bad for us. He reminds us of that in our conscience and reveals it to us through divine revelation and the teachings of the Church.

Therefore, it's up to us to learn about what's good for our souls. Our first task is to study the playbook. No excuses.

Our second task is to give 100 percent in practice. We won't be perfect from day one. No team looks the same in preseason and week fourteen of the schedule. But there is no excuse for not giving your all.

Let's look at the virtuous habits we need to be strong, smart, and pure when it comes to sexuality.

The Habit of Purity: No Time for Junk

Do your parents ask you to take out the trash every day? If they do, you know that they're asking you to do a good thing. Nobody wants stinky trash in the kitchen when the family is eating dinner! Taking out the trash keeps your house and environment clean. The same is true with your mind, will, and emotions–keeping the junk out will keep your inner self clean. The Bible calls this being pure. When you're pure and clean on the inside, not only do you feel better, but you're able to make better choices

To be pure, we must keep out the mental "junk" of impure sounds and images that bombard our senses in today's sex-focused culture. Movies, music, magazines, websites, and television shows can sometimes be good, but quite often they are part of the spiritual pollution that leads to impurity. Advertisers seem to try to get everyone's attention by using sexy images. Our world is filled with sexual images that try to destroy God's beautiful plan for men and women in marriage.

In order to stay morally strong for living God's plan, you need to be aware of the impurity in the world around you. First, try to avoid impurity whenever you can. When you do see or hear impure words, or sounds or images, be ready to turn away from it. You can resist impure temptations by refusing to think, speak, listen to, watch, or look at the twisted version of human love that breaks down the beauty of God's plan for love and sexuality in marriage. Instead, fill your mind with good stuff like learning new things or trying out new adventures.

Like an athlete in training, you say no to whatever is going to keep you from your goal. Your goal is getting to heaven and showing God's love to the world during that journey. The athlete who says no to a hot-fudge sundae because he's trying to stay in his wrestling weight class doesn't dwell too much on the sundae, or on the no. He's thinking much more about that victory he wants to earn. So should you. Saying yes to God and His plan is your focus. The no's to sin along the way are just renewals of that fundamental yes to God.

How can you keep your mind and heart purely set on God's plan for love and avoid those ideas that do not conform to His plan? It's good to set some boundaries for yourself, and then ask your parents to hold you accountable to them. Here are some practical ways that you can protect your purity:

- Use Internet controls to filter out indecency.
- Avoid "surfing" the Web and risking the chance of

running into danger on the Internet (in other words, get on the Web only when you need to, not just for fun).

- Use clean language, and choose friends who do too.
- Ask your parents to check out the movies or television shows you want to watch or books you want to read, and let them help you learn how to use good judgment for all your entertainment.

People often believe that what they see in the media is true, even if it is not! If we see anything impure on the screen committed over and over, we start to think that impurity is normal and acceptable behavior. Later, when a temptation comes along, we could more easily fall into sin rather than resist it, since we would be more familiar with the impure idea than we would be with God's beautiful plan for marriage. It's not tough to understand: Choose what strengthens you. Avoid what weakens you.

Next time you're watching a show you like, keep track of which commandments are being violated by the characters. Did someone put God last instead of first in his or her life? Did they use bad language? Talk back to his or her parents? Make fun of authority? Kill someone? Kill someone's spirit with sarcasm or put-downs? Cheat? Steal? Lie? Dress immodestly? Speak disrespectfully about sexuality? Mock God's beautiful plan for the Christian family by his or her actions? Was someone greedy?

Then ask yourself, "Why are we watching this? Is there any better entertainment we can come up with on our own? Can we find a clean comedy or adventure show?"

A winning athlete doesn't tolerate watching his sport played in an inferior way. He wants to watch and learn from the game being played at the high-est level. So should you. Watch entertainment that's going to show you what human life is all about, and what the truth of life and love really is. Life is short. You have no time for losers.

If you start to see that many of your favorite shows are offensive to God, start practicing your change-the-chan-nel-speed with the remote control, your computer mouse, or your tablet swipe. God will bless your efforts to avoid impure entertainment. He will give you the help you need to live a life of goodness and purity.

Temptations are not just on TV. There are plenty of impure Web pop-ups and sites to avoid on the Internet and other places. You may find that certain video games, mag-azines, movies, or websites invite you to sin against purity by presenting indecent pictures or scenes that can imprint themselves on your memory. You may need to avoid going to certain stores or places of recreation that could become a temptation. These are serious invitations to impurity that should be resisted. It's important first to avoid and then run from temptations of impurity. Pray for God's healing if you accidentally see something that is impure. Seek out wholesome, pure family entertainment for yourself and your friends. When your imagination wanders, fill your mind with good and pure thoughts, stories of saints and Christian heroes, great adventures, or great achievements.

No winning athlete chooses a third-rate player as a model. Keep the best role models before the eyes of your soul! With practice and repetition, you can control your thoughts and imagination to focus on the good, the true, and the beautiful.

The Habit of Purity: Friendship First

Girls sometimes go through puberty more quickly than boys their age. When a girl is maturing into a young woman, she may start acting differently toward boys. She may begin to flirt with them or try to hold hands and kiss them. Puberty is not the time for boys or girls to start developing romantic relationships. Boys sometimes start looking for girlfriends too soon as well. During puberty and the teenage years, the best kinds of relationships are friendships. When young boys and girls pair off and become "boyfriend and girl-friend," there can be sad consequences. Pairing off too soon can distract you from your schoolwork, hobbies, sports, friends, and church. Becoming romantic during the teen years most often leads to heartaches and breakups, and it can keep your personality from developing in a balanced way. During these years it's best to focus on friendships and getting to know yourself better. Learn to have fun in groups. Concentrate on loving your family and God. Follow good role models who show how to build a friendship first.

The Habit of Modesty: Private Means Private

Because of the unique and private changes taking place inside and outside your body during puberty, it's important to understand modesty and decency. Decency is a way of acting and dressing according to standards of good taste and respectability. Modesty is the choice to protect the unique and private changes going on in your body. Modesty also supports your choice to protect your manhood from mockery or misinterpretation. Instead of bragging about your muscles, or wearing shirts or pants that are too tight, you choose to cover those special and private body parts. Show-offs normally show off because they feel like they're not good enough. Modesty helps us to choose decency, which is reflected in the kinds of clothes we wear. Modesty keeps hidden what needs to be revealed only after our marriage.

We've already learned that we are all made in the image of God. That means each person is born with dignity. Each person is special and loved by God. Remember when we learned that each one of us is comprised of both body and soul? When you choose to protect the unique and hidden changes of your body by wearing attractive and decent clothing, you're saying you are proud to be a child of God! You're showing other people not just the virtuous manhood on the outside of you, but the qualities you have on the inside, too. You want people to respect you as more than just a body. You want people to see you as a body and a soul—a whole person! But sometimes people treat and look at others with disrespect. Modesty is one way of protecting yourself from being seen as just a body, or a body part, or an object. Modesty helps others see the attractive whole person you really are!

As you grow through puberty into an adult, you will learn that there are some people who do not follow God's rules or live His virtues regarding sexuality. Many people use disrespectful language when talking about their bodies or make fun of their own or other people's body parts. There are people that might use others for evil purposes or seek to harm others. If someone wants to touch one of your private body parts, or asks you to touch his or hers, it's important to say no clearly, quickly, and firmly. If someone asks you to undress for him or her so they can see your private parts, again, say no clearly, quickly, and firmly. Then get away from the situation and go tell someone about it. Do not keep secrets for people who are trying to touch you improperly or harm you or anyone else. Even if you know the person, or he or she says you are a friend, no one should be allowed to touch or look at another person's private parts. That's why we call these parts "private."

Another problem today is people taking pictures of themselves or each other that are indecent or immodest. To maintain your purity, your safety, and your reputation, *never allow this to happen*. These pictures can show up anywhere or anytime on the Internet if someone chooses to use them indecently. And once they have gone viral, they cannot be erased. Your body is a temple of the Holy Spirit, and it should be treated with reverence and respect in service of God's love.

Be careful with social media. The Internet is a broadcast medium, like television or radio; there really is nothing private on it. No matter how many controls or permissions you set, someone can search for you and find you, especially a few years from now if you're seeking a position of importance in your future job or within the community. Therefore, never put anything on the Internet that you would be uncomfortable airing on national television.

The Habit of Modesty: Dress Like a Winner

You should dress with decency and walk tall with confidence. Here are some "modesty tips" for you:

- *Dinner table*: Wear a shirt to family meals! Make sure you are completely dressed, just as if you were going to school. This lets your family know that you respect yourself, and you respect them by exercising modesty and decency.
- *Dressing up*: Show your respect for others at formal events such as awards dinners, funerals, sacraments, and Sunday Mass, first by tucking in your shirt. Be sure to find dress slacks that are not too tight or too loose. Ask your dad to help you find a good belt, nice socks, and appropriate shoes to go with your suit. You might even consider wearing a tie sometimes. Dress for an

important banquet when you to go church. After all, you are going to worship and receive God Almighty!

- *School*: Wear clean shirts and pants without holes and rips! Make sure your pants cover your underwear. Baggy pants or low-riding jeans might be acceptable to your peers, but you can make an even stronger personal statement by wearing clothing that is neat, well-fitting, and appropriate. Be careful about wearing T-shirts with slogans—not every T-shirt has a good message. Share good stuff, and look like a winner!
- *Playtime, sports, or park*: Casual clothing like T-shirts and shorts are appropriate. Sports clothing is fine, as long as it doesn't look just like your underwear.

Remember, dressing decently means knowing when to dress up and when to dress down. The clothes you wear to play in the park will be different than the clothes you wear to a family wedding. Most schools, businesses, and private clubs have dress codes that spell out standards of decency and modesty. As you become an adult, take note of the modest way respectful people dress.

Purity and Modesty in Dating

In chapter one, we learned about Marius and Cosette in *Les Misérables*. When they were old enough to date, they started spending time with each other every night in a small courtyard outside Cosette's house. (It wasn't completely honest, however, since Cosette's stepfather didn't know about it!) They shared one spontaneous kiss. Cosette was completely infatuated with Marius; she would have done anything for him. It was a dangerous situation. The author,

Victor Hugo, writes:

> Beginning with that blessed and holy hour when a kiss betrothed these two souls, Marius was there every evening. If, at that period of her existence, Cosette had fallen in love with a man in the least unscrupulous or debauched, she would have been lost; for there are generous natures which yield themselves, and Cosette was one of them. One of woman's magnanimities is to yield. Love, at the height where it is absolute, is complicated with some indescribably celestial blindness of modesty. But what dangers you run, O noble souls! Often you give the heart, and we take the body. Your heart remains with you, you gaze upon it in the gloom with a shudder. Love has no middle course; it either ruins or it saves. All human destiny lies in this dilemma. This dilemma, ruin, or safety, is set forth no more inexorably by any fatality than by love. Love is life, if it is not death. Cradle; also coffin. The same sentiment says "yes" and "no" in the human heart. Of all the things that God has made, the human heart is the one which sheds the most light, alas! and the most darkness.

God willed that Cosette's love should encounter one of the loves which save.[3]

God also wills that any girl you date should encounter a love that saves, a love that protects her and never takes advantage of a "yielding of her love," a love that respects her dignity and her purity.

If you're asking, "How far can I go, physically?" you are asking the wrong question. Would you ask your parents, "How far can I go before you kick me out of the house? That's the line I want to walk." It's insulting. It's disloyal. You're way better than that.

Back to Marius and Cosette for a moment:

Throughout the whole of the month of May of that year 1832, there were there, in every night, in that poor, neglected garden, beneath that thicket which grew thicker and more fragrant day by day, two beings composed of all chastity, all innocence, overflowing with all the felicity of heaven, nearer to the archangels than to mankind, pure, honest, intoxicated, radiant, who shone for each other amid the shadows. It seemed to Cosette that Marius had a crown, and to Marius that Cosette had a nimbus. They touched each other, they gazed at each other, they clasped each other's hands, they pressed close to each other; but there was a distance which they did not pass. Not that they respected it; they did not know of its existence. Marius was conscious of a barrier, Cosette's innocence; and Cosette of a support, Marius' loyalty. The first kiss had also been the last. Marius, since that time, had not gone further than to touch Cosette's hand, or her kerchief, or a lock of her hair, with his lips. For him, Cosette was a perfume and not a woman. He inhaled her. She refused nothing, and he asked nothing. Cosette was happy, and Marius was satisfied. They lived in this ecstatic state which can be described as the dazzling of one soul by another soul.[4]

Any girl a guy happens to date deserves to be able to count on his loyalty. If she turns out to be less than innocent and welcomes physical advances, he must stay loyal to what he knows is best for her and for himself. In that case, he should end the relationship, because if she puts him in danger by offering temptation, she is not looking out for what's best for him. She is helping him lose the battle of life and love. Life is too short to deal with losers or those who want to make us losers.

Accept the Challenge

The actions you choose with your mind and do with your body should always show that you love God, love yourself, and love your family and friends. God created girls and women to be beautiful on the outside and pure on the inside. He designed feminine beauty to attract others to God in good ways. God created boys and men to be masculine on the outside and pure on the inside. God placed in both men and women a desire to be loved by God and loved by their family and friends. That is how we can reflect the goodness of God through our whole self—body and soul.

Why take the "Purity Challenge? Why would you need to do this? Because the sight, sound, or smell of a beautiful woman can take over your imagination and easily lead to lustful thoughts or the idea that she is an object for pleasure. A man with a pure mind and heart trains himself to see the beauty of a young woman made in the likeness and image of God, a person who deserves respect.

It will take some practice, when the new hormones begin to flow, for you to see a woman's inner beauty and not to be distracted by her body. Men are naturally wired to respond to visual attraction. It's definitely easier to see a woman's dignity when she dresses with dignity. However, not all young women dress modestly these days. Unfortunately, immodesty is all around us. It may be that you need to look away, say a prayer, or think of your favorite sport or some other interest when faced with a difficult situation. Remember that speedy remote control channel changer for your TV and that delete button on your electronic devices? Use them whenever needed to protect your pure mind.

Be confident and walk with God. "I have the strength for everything through him who empowers me" (Phil 4:13). God has given you everything you need to be good, modest, and pure. You have what it takes. Be assured by His grace.

Building your character in manhood is up to you. God gives you the body and the soul, but you have to do the work. The virtue of chastity takes practice, and there will be many temptations to sin against chastity that you will need to avoid. Remember, chastity is the virtue that directs your manhood toward authentic love and away from using people. The virtue of chastity will help you to keep your thoughts and experiences of romantic love pure and according to God's plan for you. In today's world, a young man needs to do all he can to avoid sins against chastity.

The ninth commandment states, "You shall not covet your neighbor's wife" (Ex 20:17). This includes any woman, even if she is not married. In this day and age, we need also to remind women to avoid lusting after men or seeing them as objects instead of persons. And Jesus said, "Everyone who looks at a woman with lust has already committed adultery with her in his heart" (Mt 5:28). Lust destroys love. Lust is the opposite of sexual self-control; it's acting on your feelings rather than acting according to God's plan for love. Christ's warnings about lust are an invitation to a pure way of looking at others, a way of controlling our thoughts, and a way to respect women by seeing them as friends and treasured daughters of God.

Hitting the Pavement

All of this is fine in theory, but there are some very concrete things you can do that will help you to maintain the necessary virtue of chastity during these important teen years so you can be pure and a total gift of self for your future wife and for God. Here are a few:

- Do you have a family computer? Try putting that computer in a very visible place, with the screen facing everyone who walks into the room.
- Do you have a personal computer, laptop, smartphone, or tablet? Ask your parents to put filters on them.
- Get drastic! Challenge yourself and your family: Turn off all of the personal electronic devices and computers in the house at a designated time in the evening. Just *be* together as a family, enjoying interesting conversations, laughing, and having fun.

- One day per week, instead of electronic entertainment, play a board game or interactive game that spurs on conversation or creativity with your family members, or do something active such as take a hike together or have a scavenger hunt.
- Improve your communication skills by texting less and having more real conversations. You might even try writing an old-fashioned letter to a friend or relative. Spend time with people while none of you are in front of a TV, phone, or computer screen. Talk, listen, love.
- Do you have cable or satellite TV? Ask your parents to put filters on it to keep out indecency.
- Instead of having a TV in every room, suggest that your family sell all of the TVs except for one in your living room or den. Use the money from selling the extra TVs to go out together for a special dinner or some other treat—or put the money in a vacation fund.
- If it's offered, take a family computer safety class at your local church or recreation center.
- Talk with your parents about the music you and your friends listen to. Let them hear samples on YouTube or other sites so they can help you decide whether that music is helping you to be pure. Do the lyrics express good thoughts about truth, beauty, and the goodness of life?
  - Talk about your favorite song. Does this song make you think about truth and goodness? Does the song remind you of the beauty of life and God's creation?
  - Are all the words in the song decent and respectful?

- Is the singer a person who is decent and respectful? Is the music video respectful of the dignity of the human person?
- Choose to put only those good sounds into your head.

Natural and Supernatural Help

No victorious athlete is born that way. It takes hard work, training, and habits. It also takes coaching and the support of teammates. In your battle to be faithful to God's plan for victory in your life, we just covered some habits you need to form.

Along with the Purity Challenge, here are some things that can help you practice the virtue of chastity:

- *Exercise and work*: A lot of sexual temptation comes from pent-up energy. Stay active. If you're too much of a couch potato, you're probably exposing yourself to too many temptations through TV, computer, or video games. Get some fresh air; play sports, even if you're not going to play varsity. Do some hard physical work outside. This all helps keep you focused on noble things.
- *Good friendships*: If the crew you run with is bringing you down, you need to bail and find better friends. A friend wants what's best for you. You want to be around people who agree with what's best. And you have to be a good friend, too. Help your friends protect purity and modesty. As bad as it is to fall into sin, it's even worse to lead someone else into sin. You don't want to face God with that on your conscience.
- *Be a man for others*: Impurity is a danger when we focus on ourselves. Do things that bring you out of

yourself to focus on the good of others. Volunteer, help the poor, or get involved in a parish youth group. Don't think of service hours as a box you have to check for some requirement. Focusing on the needs of others is one of the main habits you will need as a husband and father someday. Start early to get all the experience you can at putting others first.

- *Frequent confession*: The Sacrament of Reconciliation is absolutely necessary. That's why Jesus set it up for us. Frequent confession helps keep us honest and gives us the grace we need to be strong. It's real strength from above. Every two weeks or every month—speak with your confessor (you should go to the same priest as consistently as possible); he will help you see how often is best for you. You should clean out your soul about as often as you clean out your room. And that should be every month at least!

- *Mom and Dad*: When you pull away from the family a bit as you make friends, or even feel the pull of the romantic circle, don't write off your Mom and Dad. Your relationship with them will not be the same as when you were little, but it's great to start to relate to your dad on more of a man-to-man level. Just remember, he's been where you are and lived to tell the tale. Don't harbor secrets. If you have a question about something, ask it.

So now you've seen God's plan in nature, His supernatural plan, and what you have to do to execute His plan. It's time to get on the field and start working for victory.

But since this is not just a game but life, and life is in God's hands, what you first need to do—and often—is to turn to Him and ask for His divine help.

Discussion Questions

Answer and discuss these questions with your Dad.

1. In what area of your life do you give 100 percent: sports, friends, schoolwork, chores, obeying your parents? Which area should you give more than you already do?

_____

_____

_____

2. What practices can you incorporate into your life to help you become stronger on the inside and the outside? What should you avoid because it makes you weaker?

_____

_____

_____

3. Read the first quote from *Les Misérables* found in the "Purity and Modesty in Dating" section. Discuss two messages about romantic love that it contains.

_____

_____

_____

4. In the second quote in that section, notice how Marius was able to keep a loving distance from Cosette to

show how much he loved and respected her. What should a man do to "keep a loving distance" from a girl he loves in order to practice self-control in a tempting situation?

_____

_____

_____

5. "Chastity is the virtue that directs our sexuality and sexual desires toward authentic love and away from using others for sexual pleasure" (*Catechetical Formation in Chaste Living*, p. 7, USCCB, 2008). Review what this means to you now.

_____

_____

_____

Chapter Reflections

While discussing this chapter, my Dad gave me some extra advice about . . .

_____

_____

_____

While reading this chapter, I learned these two important things:

1. _____

2. _____

I resolve to live out the *LoveEd* teachings from this chapter by . . .

_____

_____

_____

Finish this chapter with the following prayer:
Jesus, I want to be strong, smart, and pure like You and like all the saints. Thank You for the Church to guide me and my family and teachers to lead me on the path to real love here on earth and towards eternal love with You. Amen.

My Dad and I completed this chapter on

_____

(date and time)

CHAPTER 6

Pure Power from Above

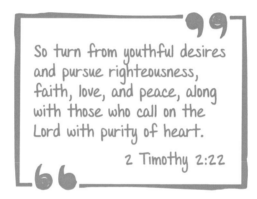

So turn from youthful desires and pursue righteousness, faith, love, and peace, along with those who call on the Lord with purity of heart.

2 Timothy 2:22

The information in these chapters has been a lot to take in. You may be feeling tired or overwhelmed. Maybe you feel conflicted because you haven't been living according to God's plan. The season is far from over, though; victory can still be yours!

A coach and a team spend time after each game to watch game film. They ask what went right and what went wrong. It's not a time to blame someone for dropping a pass, even though that receiver may have to watch himself mess up in front of the whole team. The focus is on improvement. It's about getting better together.

Michael has learned to review the game film of his day. In dialogue with God, his head coach, he reviews the positives and negatives and plans for a better game when he takes the field of life tomorrow.

He exercised with his brother Joey: "Lord, thanks for helping me take care of my body and be a good brother to Joey. Thanks for letting me share my love of sports with him and teach him to throw a football. Please make his fingers grow fast so he can grip the laces better!"

He refused the offer of a cigarette: "Lord, help me to keep saying no to things that harm the health You've given me. And help me be a good example without being too 'preachy' about it. Next time help me say something like 'No, I prefer to have my lungs when I'm fifty. . . .'"

He admired his dad and his work ethic: "Lord, give me the grace to always follow good examples. Thanks for my dad. Help me to pray for him more and all the challenges he faces as a man these days."

He was in a situation where someone was doing something inappropriate on his phone: "Lord, I am sorry I even looked at that image on the phone. I will confess that in confession. Forgive me. I want to see women in a pure light. Thanks for giving me the grace to walk away. Help me to see temptations to impurity like a snake in my path and just run away from them. St. Michael, defend me in this battle. You are the dragon slayer! Next time maybe I should say something. Help me to be brave and say, 'Dude, that's lame. That's someone's daughter, someone's sister. How would you feel if that was your sister? That's beneath us. We are better than that.'"

He wavered about coming home on time, especially when he had his first real conversation with Julia and his heart was pounding a mile a minute: "Lord, help me to remember that when I obey my parents I am obeying You. Thanks for helping me get home on time—sorry to cut it that close. Also, thanks for letting me not look like too much of a fool in front of Julia. I really like her. You know that—You know everything. Help me to stay focused. I think You're calling me to marriage, unless You send me some clear clues about some other vocation. I know I can't get married tomorrow, so please help me stay chaste and pure to give my future wife that whole gift of self, just like You gave Your whole life for us on the Cross. By the way, is my future wife Julia? . . . *silence* . . . Okay, a good coach never makes it too easy for his players. I get it. Just help me follow Your game plan always in my life. Lord, I love You and want to share Your victory. Tomorrow, with Your help, I promise to make an effort to obey my parents more promptly."

A game film of your day—that's what an examination of conscience is. You should do one especially when you prepare for confession, but you should also do one every night before you go to bed. Examine before God what went right and what went wrong. If things went right, thank God and see how you can continue along that road. If you fumbled, don't dwell on it. Take responsibility for it and ask God's help for the future. But also ask for light to see ways you can avoid failing in the future.

All sins harm our souls, but some kill it. That's why they are called "mortal" (think mortal wound). If we've done something seriously wrong, and we knew it was wrong, and we consented to it, we have killed the life of God in our souls. We need to get to confession as soon as reasonably possible.

All sexual matters are serious. As we have seen, sex has to do with the inner depth of our calling to show God's love to the world through a complete gift of ourselves. It is central to God's plan.

There are some good guides out there for conscience exams. Ask your parents or your confessor for one that suits you.

The Power of a Champion

When a Roman general won a huge victory, he was granted a "Triumph." This was a holiday with a parade and the general processing in a chariot with the spoils of war and treasures captured, and prisoners, his enemies, in chains.

In His passion and death, Jesus won the ultimate victory over sin and death. His resurrection is the greatest triumph ever. That is what we celebrate at every Mass. One of those graces is the power to put His enemies in chains. We need to rely on God's power and trust Him. We also need to get in the habit of asking for it.

As we finish our presentation of what it means to be strong, smart, and pure, plan to spend some time with God, thank Him, and ask Him for His help.

Since you're reading this with your parents—above

all with your Dad–this is something you should each do individually.

Each of you should find a quiet place where you won't be interrupted for about fifteen minutes. Think of it as a pre-game pep talk from the greatest coach in the world: your heavenly Father.

Pure Power Prayer: A Meditation for You

Put yourself in God's presence. He is everywhere, so He is with you now. He is in the world He created, and He is in the soul He created. He dwells in your soul through sanctifying grace. Ask Him to help you to be aware of Him, to live each day knowing He is always with you.

Consider how awesome God is. Put yourself on that spaceship flying to Pluto. Look out the window as you travel thousands of miles an hour. "God, you made all of this! Wow." Spend some time telling God how amazing He is to have created all of this. This is the way to praise Him.

Think of God who, being so immense, thought of you when you were nothing. He brought your parents together and formed your body in your mother's womb. He personally created your soul, with your ability to share in His knowing and loving. Marvel at yourself as God's self-portrait.

You might want to use the words of this psalm:

You formed my inmost being;
You knit me in my mother's womb.
I praise you, because I am wonderfully made;
wonderful are your works!
My very self you know.
My bones are not hidden from you,
When I was being made in secret,
fashioned in the depths of the earth.

Your eyes saw me unformed;
in your book all are written down;
my days were shaped, before one came to be.
How precious to me are your designs, O God;
how vast the sum of them!
(Ps 139:13-17)

Thank God for the examples you have in your own family circle of love. Thank Him for your parents, for their love for each other, for their strength in dealing with their own struggles, for how they welcomed you into life, for their generosity and patience with you. Thank Him for each of your siblings and for the members of your extended family. Ask for His help to always see them as a gift from Him.

Talk to God about all the changes that are happening in your life. Thank Him for the changes in your body, all according to His plan. Thank Him for designing everything so amazingly. Thank Him for giving you the mission of showing His love to the world through the total gift of yourself.

Thank Him for your friends by name. Ask for His help to be a good friend and always to lead them closer to Him. Thank Him for the good times you have. Ask forgiveness for any times you have failed to have your friends' best interests at heart, for any bad examples you have given, for any times you have led them into sin. Ask for God's strength to promise never again to put your own friends in danger of sin.

Thank Him for creating us male and female. Thank Him for being a guy, for the natural talents and strengths that go along with it. Thank Him for making girls, for all that you can learn from them and admire in them. Ask Him for His grace to be a good friend to girls, to protect them and respect them and never see them as objects for pleasure, but instead to view them as royal princesses adopted into God's family. Ask forgiveness for any times you have failed to respect them or have consented to impure thoughts or otherwise treated them as objects rather than as persons and temples of God.

Ask Him for guidance as you grow older and stronger and begin to have romantic feelings. Ask Him to follow the example of St. Joseph, such a great man, in his chaste love for Our Lady. Ask to be like a knight, always willing to champion a girl's virtue.

Ask for light about your vocation. If you feel called to the priesthood or consecrated life, thank God for that thought. Ask for His help to stay pure in preparation for a life of celibacy and dedication to others. Pray for your future flock, the souls you will bring closer to Christ.

If you feel called to marriage, thank God for that thought. Ask God's help to stay pure in preparation for giving yourself totally to your future wife. Pray for her. She's out there. Ask God for His grace to help find her when the time is right. Ask Him to be able to love her like He does, to lay down your life for her like Jesus did. Promise never to do anything that would make you a less worthy husband.

Lift up your heart toward God and, whether or not any feelings or emotions accompany this prayer, bring your will into it. Tell the Lord that you want to follow His plan, that you want to embrace all the sacrifice that is needed to achieve victory and share His glory.

Ask for light to see if there is one concrete thing you can do today to follow God's plan of love better—one concrete thing. Ask God to remind you throughout the day. Consider writing it down. You can review it tonight when you examine your conscience.

Ask Our Lady, your Mother in heaven, to help you and

intercede for you. Ask her to ask God for His grace for you to be able to follow His plan now and until the hour of your death.

End by praying an Our Father, a Hail Mary and a Glory Be, offering your day to God in a sincere gift of yourself.

Game Time!

Well done.

You're on your way to being strong, smart, and pure. You're familiar with the playbook; you know what's at stake. You know what habits you need to form. You know what these changes in your life mean.

Most importantly, you've asked God for light and grace. He wants to give them to you. Renew this pure power prayer often, each day if you can.

Life is right out there, waiting for you. It's game time. Be a champion of God's plan of love and share with Him the glory of victory!

Give the book to your Dad now, so he can read the next section himself. Tell him you'll meet him in fifteen minutes. Then go ask your Mom if there's anything you can do for her.

Pure Power Prayer: A Meditation for Dad

Dad, don't skimp on this. Your son's future happiness may depend on it.

Put yourself in God's presence. He is everywhere, so He is with you now. He is in the world He created, and He is in the soul He created. He dwells in your soul through sancti-fying grace. Ask Him to help you to be aware of Him, to live each day knowing He is always with you.

Maybe it's been a while since you considered God's awesomeness. Thank Him that He is using this opportunity to bring you closer to Him. You have an amazing project in common: this incredible son He has given you. He has entrusted him to you so you can lead him along the pathways of God's plan. By following this program you have renewed your own knowledge of this plan.

Thank God for your own parents and for their sacrifice and dedication. Forgive them from your heart if there were shortcomings. If they have passed away, commend their souls to God. If they are still alive, thank God for their continued help in your life.

Thank God for your wife. Thank Him for her love and for the amazing vocation of marriage. Ask that your marriage be strong, that it can show the world the love of God in the Trinity, that your self-giving to each other can be an imitation of Christ's self-giving to His Church. Ask Him to be able to rediscover each day what made you fall in love with her. Even though romantic feelings come and go, ask Him for the resolve to be her champion always. If you're struggling with any marital problems, ask God's forgiveness for any part you have had in them, and promise God you will do all in your power to overcome them, in service to Him and to your family. Ask for the grace to put your family first—ahead of career, ahead of selfish interests, ahead of everything.

Thank God for this vocation to marriage. Thank Him for your faithfulness to your family, which is your faithfulness to Him. Thank Him for so many concrete ways to show your love for Him by your love for your wife and family.

Thank God for your friends, too. School buddies, work colleagues. Ask Him for the grace to be a good friend, and above all never to do anything that would separate them from God. If you have ever given bad example or led them to sin, ask God's forgiveness (and plan on going to confession soon if needed).

Ask for forgiveness if you've ever seen religion as "a woman thing." Look at the crucifix . . . "Behold the Man." That's your model as a man. Are you willing to go the distance for your wife and family? Are you willing to make a total gift of yourself every day for them?

Thank God for your kids, especially for this wondrous boy with whom you did this program. Think about all the God-given goodness in him, all his talents. Think of how God the Father must feel when He sees him, knowing all the good He created in him and all the great things he is capable of. Ask forgiveness if you have ever neglected him or led him astray, or if you have been indifferent to him or put work or other concerns before him. Promise God that you will be as steadfast with him as St. Joseph was for Jesus, teaching him what is true and good and beautiful.

Ask forgiveness if you have committed any sins against purity. Promise God that you will make your house a fortress of virtue and of goodness. Promise to be vigilant and protect your family from all the enemies that lurk and wish to harm their souls. Beg forgiveness if your bad example in this area has had a negative effect on your family. Decide here and now to clean up your act and, with God's help, rebuild your house to be a bastion of purity and goodness. Ask God's help to be demanding about this, without making compromises with worldly ideas that can leave your wife and children unprotected against the enemies of their souls.

Thank God for the great trust He has given you by making you the head of a family. Beg God once again for His grace and His protection for you to lead your family to heaven.

If any part of this book has convicted you, if you have seen that improvements can and should be made, ask God for the power to bring them to fruition. Ask for forgiveness if you have been a spiritual weakling.

Make a commitment before God to be the husband your wife needs you to be, to help her become the saint God created her to be, and to be the kind of dad your son needs so that he too can become a saint.

Ask for light to see if there is one concrete thing you can do today to follow God's plan of love better—one concrete thing. Ask God to remind you throughout the day. Perhaps write it down. You can review it tonight when you examine your conscience.

Ask Our Lady, your Mother in heaven, to help you and intercede for you. Ask her to ask God for His grace so that you can follow His plan now and until the hour of your death.

In closing, read Luke 2:41-52 with your son. This passage is about Jesus when he was twelve years old. Discuss why it is important to always obey God the Father in order to grow in wisdom and in grace.

End by praying an Our Father, a Hail Mary and a Glory Be, offering your day to God in a sincere gift of yourself.

Now give that son of yours a big bear hug, tell him you love him, and make a promise together to dedicate yourselves to being strong, smart, and pure.

Endnotes

1. St. Augustine, Confessions, Book III, chapter 6.

2. Puebla, Mexico. Homily, Sunday, 28 January 1979. www.vatican.va.

3. Victor Hugo, Les Misérables, translated by Isabel Hapgood, Book 8, Chapter 1 (Thomas Crowell and Co: New York, 1887); e-book. http://www.gutenberg.org/files/135/135-h/135-h.htm.

4. Ibid.

Notes

Notes

Notes